C. C. W. Taylor

SOCRATES

A Very Short Introduction

OXFORD
UNIVERSITY PRESS

OXFORD
UNIVERSITY PRESS

Great Clarendon Street, Oxford OX2 6DP

Oxford University Press is a department of the University of Oxford.
It furthers the University's objective of excellence in research, scholarship,
and education by publishing worldwide in

Oxford New York

Auckland Bangkok Buenos Aires Cape Town Chennai
Dar es Salaam Delhi Hong Kong Istanbul Karachi Kolkata
Kuala Lumpur Madrid Melbourne Mexico City Mumbai Nairobi
São Paulo Shanghai Taipei Tokyo Toronto

Oxford is a registered trade mark of Oxford University Press
in the UK and in certain other countries

Published in the United States
by Oxford University Press Inc., New York

First published 1998
First published as a Very Short Introduction 2000

British Library Cataloguing in Publication Data
Data available

Library of Congress Cataloging in Publication Data
Data available
ISBN 978-0-19-285412-4

14 16 18 20 19 17 15 13

Typeset by RefineCatch Ltd, Bungay, Suffolk
Printed in Great Britain by
Ashford Colour Press Ltd, Gosport, Hampshire

Contents

List of Illustrations

The publisher and the author apologize for any errors or omissions in the above list. If contacted they will be pleased to rectify these at the earliest opportunity.

Acknowledgements

Anyone who writes on Socrates must acknowledge his or her indebtedness to the very large amount of scholarly work on that philosopher, most of it written in the later part of the twentieth century, and much of it of the highest quality. We are all part of a continuing tradition. Details of some of the most significant modern work on Socrates are given in the section on Further Reading at the end of this book.

In addition to this general indebtedness, certain portions of this book borrow heavily from specific writings by others. The first section in Chapter 2, 'Authors other than Plato', relies particularly on D. Clay, 'The Origins of the Socratic Dialogue', in P. A. Vander Waerdt (ed.), *The Socratic Movement* (Ithaca, NY and London, 1994) and on C. H. Kahn, *Plato and the Socratic Dialogue* (Cambridge, 1996), ch. 1. Chapter 5, 'Socrates and Later Philosophy', relies on a number of authors: in the section on 'Ancient Philosophy' I am indebted above all to A. A. Long, 'Socrates in Hellenistic Philosophy', *Classical Quarterly*, 38 (1988), 150–71, and also to contributions to Vander Waerdt's *The Socratic Movement* by G. Striker, J. G. DeFillipo and P. T. Mitsis, J. Annas, and V. T. McKirahan. (Details of those articles may be found in that volume.) The section 'Medieval and Modern Philosophy' is based in part on P. J. Fitzpatrick, 'The Legacy of Socrates', in B. S. Gower and M. C. Stokes (eds.), *Socratic Questions* (London and New York, 1992).

Abbreviations

DL	Diogenes Laertius
Pl.	Plato
Apol.	*Apology* (*Defence of Socrates*)
Charm.	*Charmides*
Euthyd.	*Euthydemus*
Euthyph.	*Euthyphro*
Gorg.	*Gorgias*
Hipp. Ma.	*Hippias Major*
Lach.	*Laches*
Ph.	*Phaedo*
Prot.	*Protagoras*
Rep.	*Republic*
Symp.	*Symposium*
Tht.	*Theaetetus*
Xen.	Xenophon
Apol.	*Apology*
Mem.	*Memorabilia*
Oec.	*Oeconomicus*
Symp.	*Symposium*

Chapter 1
Introduction

Socrates has a unique position in the history of philosophy. On the one hand he is one of the most influential of all philosophers, and on the other one of the most elusive and least known. Further, his historical influence is not itself independent of his elusiveness. First we have the influence of the actual personality of Socrates on his contemporaries, and in particular on Plato. It is no exaggeration to say that had it not been for the impact on him of the life and above all of the death of Socrates Plato would probably have become a statesman rather than a philosopher, with the result that the whole development of Western philosophy would have been unimaginably different. Then we have the enduring influence of the figure of Socrates as an exemplar of the philosophic life, of a total moral and intellectual integrity permeating every detail of everyday life and carried to the heroic extreme of steadfastness in the face of rejection and ignominious death. But the figure of Socrates the protomartyr and patron saint of philosophy, renewed in every age to speak to that age's philosophical condition, is the creation, not of the man himself, but of those who wrote about him, above all of Plato. It is Plato's depiction of the ideal philosopher which has fascinated and inspired from his day to ours, and if we attempt to penetrate that depiction in the quest for the historical Socrates we find the latter as elusive as the historical Jesus of nineteenth-century New Testament scholarship.

Again, there are two main reasons for this elusiveness (a situation which reinforces the scriptural parallel). First, Socrates wrote nothing himself, and secondly (and consequently), after his death he quickly became the subject of a literary genre, that of 'Socratic conversations' (*Sōkratikoi logoi*), in which various of his associates presented imaginative representations of his conversations, representations which focused on different aspects of his personality and style of conversation in accordance with the particular interests of the individual author. Plato's dialogues and the Socratic writings of Xenophon are the only examples of this genre to survive complete, while scraps of other Socratic writings, notably those of Aeschines, survive through quotation by later authors. This literature will be discussed in more detail below. For the moment it should be emphasized that, while each of Plato, Xenophon, and the rest presents his own picture of Socrates in line with his particular purpose, each presents a picture *of Socrates*. That is to say, it would be a serious distortion to think of any of these writers as creating a free-standing figure, for example, of the ideal philosopher, or the model citizen, to which figure its author attaches the name 'Socrates'. Socrates is, indeed, depicted by Plato as the ideal philosopher, and in my view that depiction involves at various stages the attribution to him of philosophical doctrines which Plato knew that Socrates never maintained, for the very good reason that Plato had himself invented those doctrines after Socrates' death. But Socrates was in Plato's view the appropriate paradigm of the ideal philosopher because of the kind of person Plato believed Socrates to have been, and the kind of life Plato believed him to have lived. In the sense in which the terms 'fiction' and 'biography' designate exclusive categories, 'Socratic conversations' are neither works of fiction nor works of biography. They express their authors' responses to their understanding of the personality of a unique individual and to the events of that individual's life, and in order to understand them we must seek to make clear what is known, or at least reasonably believed, about that personality and those events.

1. Bust of Socrates – a Roman copy of an original made shortly after Socrates' death.

Chapter 2
Life

While Socrates' death can be firmly fixed by the record of his trial to the early spring of 399 BC (Athenian official year 400/399), there is an unimportant dispute about the precise date of his birth. The second-century BC chronicler Apollodorus (cited by the third-century AD biographer Diogenes Laertius (2.44)) assigns it with unusual precision (even giving his birthday) to early May 468 (towards the end of the Athenian official year 469/8) but Plato twice (*Apol.* 17d, *Crito* 52e) has Socrates describe himself as seventy years old at the time of his trial. So, either Socrates, still in his sixty-ninth year, is to be taken generously as describing himself as getting on for seventy, or (as most scholars assume) the Apollodoran date (probably arrived at by counting back inclusively seventy years from 400/399) is one or two years late. The official indictment (quoted by Diogenes Laertius) names his father, Sophroniscus, and his deme or district, Alopeke (just south of the city of Athens), and in Plato's *Theaetetus* (149a) he gives his mother's name as Phainarete and says that she was a strapping midwife. That may well have been true, though the appropriateness of the name (whose literal sense is 'revealing virtue') and profession to Socrates' self-imposed task of acting as midwife to the ideas of others (*Tht.* 149–51) suggests the possibility of literary invention. His father was said to have been a stonemason, and there is a tradition that Socrates himself practised that trade for some time; the fact that he served in the heavy infantry, who had to supply their own weapons and armour, indicates that his circumstances were reasonably prosperous. His ascetic life-style was more probably an expression of a philosophical position than the reflection of real poverty. His wife was Xanthippe, celebrated by Xenophon and others (though not by Plato) for her bad temper. They had three sons, two of them small children at the time of Socrates' death; evidently her difficult temper, if real, was not an obstacle to the continuation of conjugal relations into Socrates' old age. An unreliable later tradition, implausibly ascribed to Aristotle, mentions a second wife named Myrto, marriage to whom is variously described as preceding, following, or bigamously coinciding with the marriage to Xanthippe.

Virtually nothing is known of the first half of his life. He is reported to have been the pupil of Archelaus, an Athenian, himself a pupil of Anaxagoras; Archelaus' interests included natural philosophy and ethics (according to Diogenes Laertius 'he said that there are two causes of coming into being, hot and cold, and that animals come to be from slime and that the just and the disgraceful exist not by nature but by convention' (2.16)). The account of Socrates' early interest in natural philosophy put into his mouth in Plato's *Phaedo* (96a ff.) may reflect this stage in his development; if so, he soon shifted his interest to other areas, while any influence in ethics on the part of Archelaus can only have been negative.

It is only with the outbreak of the Peloponnesian War in 432, when he was already over 35, that he begins to emerge onto the historical scene. Plato several times (*Apol.* 28e, *Charm.* 153a, and *Symp.* 219e ff.) refers to his military service at the siege of Potidaea on the north Aegean coast in the opening years of the war, and in the last of these passages has Alcibiades enlarge on his courage in combat and his remarkable endurance of the ferocious winter conditions, in which he went about wearing his ordinary (by implication, thin) clothing and barefoot. The latter detail is of interest in linking Plato's portrayal of Socrates with our only unambiguously independent evidence for his

2. A comical representation of Socrates with his 'two wives', by the 17th-century Dutch painter Caesar Boethius van Everdingen (1606–78). The stone on which Socrates is leaning bears the maxim 'Know Thyself', inscribed on the temple of Apollo at Delphi, which was treated in antiquity as a Socratic slogan.

personality and activity, the portrayal of him in fifth-century comedy. Some lines of the comic dramatist Ameipsias, quoted (according to most scholars, from his lost play *Connus*, which was placed above Aristophanes' *Clouds* in the competition of 423) by Diogenes Laertius, refer to his physical endurance, his ostentatiously simple clothing, and his going barefoot 'to spite the shoemakers'; and shoelessness is twice mentioned as a Socratic trademark in *Clouds* (103, 363). Another comic poet, Eupolis, referred to him as a beggarly chatterbox, who didn't know where his next meal was coming from, and as a thief, another detail reproduced in Aristophanes' caricature (*Clouds* 177–9). By the 420s, then, Socrates was sufficiently well known to be a figure of fun for his eccentrically simple life-style and for his loquacity. But, while his individual characteristics undoubtedly provided welcome comic material, it is as representative of a number of important and, in the dramatist's eyes, unwelcome trends in contemporary life that he figures in the only dramatic portrayal to have survived, that in Aristophanes' *Clouds*.

The crucial point is well summarized by W. K. C. Guthrie:

> [W]e can recognize in the Socrates of the *Clouds* at least three different types which were never united to perfection in any single person: first the Sophist, who teaches the art of making a good case out of a bad one; secondly the atheistic natural philosopher like Anaxagoras; and thirdly the ascetic moral teacher, ragged and starving through his own indifference to worldly interests.[1]

In the play Socrates presides over an institution where students pay to learn techniques of chicanery to avoid paying their debts; this is called 'making the weaker argument defeat the stronger', a slogan associated with the sophist Protagoras, and the combat between the two arguments, in which the conventional morality of the stronger (also identified as the Just Argument) succumbs to the sophistry of the weaker (the Unjust Argument), is a central scene of the play. But, as well as a teacher of sophistry, the Socrates of the *Clouds* is a natural philosopher with a special interest in the study of the heavens, a study which involves rejection of traditional religion and its divinization of the heavenly bodies in favour of the new deities: Air, Aither, Clouds, Chaos, Tongue, and 'heavenly swirl', which displaces Zeus as the supreme power of the universe. Naturally, the new 'religion' provides the metaphysical underpinning of the sophistical immoralism, since, unlike the traditional gods (who are not 'current coin with us', as Socrates says (247–8)), the new deities have no interest in punishing wrongdoers. At the conclusion of the play Socrates' house is burnt down specifically as a punishment for the impious goings-on which have taken place in it; 'investigating the position of (peering at the arse of) the moon' and 'offering wicked violence to the gods' (1506–9) are two sides of the same coin.

By 423, then, Socrates was sufficiently well known to be caricatured as a representative of the new learning as it appeared to conservatively minded Athenians, a subversive cocktail of scientific speculation and argumentative gymnastics, with alarming implications for conventional morality and religion. Such a burlesque does not, of course, imply detailed knowledge on the part of either dramatist or audience of the doctrines or activities either of Socrates or of contemporary intellectuals (though a number of commentators have been impressed by parallels between details of the doctrines ridiculed in *Clouds* and some of the doctrines of the contemporary natural philosopher Diogenes of Apollonia). But both dramatist and audience must have had some picture (allowing for a great deal of exaggeration, oversimplification, and distortion) of what sort of thing Socrates on the one hand and 'intellectuals' like Protagoras and Diogenes on the other were getting up to. We have to ask what Socrates had done by 423 to create that picture.

It is totally implausible that he had actually done what Aristophanes represents him as doing, namely, set up a residential institution for

8

scientific research and tuition in argumentative techniques, or even that he had received payment for teaching in any of these areas. Both Plato and Xenophon repeatedly and emphatically deny that Socrates claimed scientific expertise or taught for money (*Apol.* 19d–20c, 31b–c, Xen. *Mem.* 1.2.60, 1.6.5, and 1.6.13), and the contrast between the professional sophist, who amasses great wealth (*Meno* 91d, *Hipp. Ma.* 282d–e) as a 'pedlar of goods for the soul' (*Prot.* 313c), and Socrates, who gives his time freely to others out of concern for their welfare and lives in poverty in consequence (*Apol.* 31b–c), is a central theme in Plato's distancing of the two. It is impossible to believe that Plato (and to a lesser extent Xenophon) would have systematically engaged on that strategy in the knowledge that Socrates was already notorious as exactly such a huckster of learning, but not at all difficult to believe that comic distortion depicts him as such when he was in fact something else. What else? One thing every depiction of Socrates agrees on is that he was, above all, an arguer and questioner, who went about challenging people's pretensions to expertise and revealing inconsistencies in their beliefs. That was the sort of thing that sophists were known, or at least believed, to do, and, for a fee, to teach others to do. It was, therefore, easy for Socrates, who was in any case conspicuous for his threadbare coat (*Prot.* 335d, Xen. *Mem*. 1.6.2, DL 2.28 (citing Ameipsias)), lack of shoes, and peculiar swaggering walk (*Clouds* 362, Pl. *Symp.* 221b), to become 'That oddball Socrates who goes about arguing with everyone and catching them out; one of those sophist fellows, with their damned tricky arguments, telling people there aren't any gods but air and swirl, and that the sun's a red-hot stone, and rubbish of that kind.' Rumours of his early interest in natural philosophy and association with Archelaus and (possibly) of unconventional religious attitudes may have filled out the picture, which the comic genius of Aristophanes brought to life on the stage in 423.

Plato mentions two other episodes of active military service at Delium in Boeotia in 424 (*Apol.* 28e, *Lach.* 181a, and *Symp.* 221a–b) and at

Amphipolis on the north Aegean coast in 422 (*Apol.* 28e). His courage during the retreat from Delium became legendary, and later writers report that he saved Xenophon's life on that occasion. As Xenophon was about six years old at the time the incident is obviously fictitious, doubtless derived from Alcibiades' account of Socrates' heroism in the earlier campaign at Potidaea, which included his saving Alcibiades' life when he was wounded (*Symp.* 220d-e). At any rate, it is clear that exceptional physical courage was an element in the accepted picture of Socrates, along with indifference to physical hardship, a remarkable capacity to hold his liquor (*Symp.* 214a, 220a, 223c-d), and, in some accounts, a strongly passionate temperament, in which anger and sexual desire were kept under restraint by reason (Cicero, *Tusculan Disputations*, 4.37.80, cf. Pl. *Charm.* 155c-e, *Symp.* 216d) (or were not, according to the hostile Aristoxenus). We are given a detailed picture of his physical appearance in middle age in Xenophon's *Symposium*, where he describes himself as snub-nosed, with wide nostrils, protruding eyes, thick lips (5.5-7), and a paunch (2.19), which exactly fits Alcibiades' description of him in Plato's *Symposium* as like a satyr or Silenus (215b, 216d; cf. Xen. *Symp.* 4.19). (For the snub nose and protruding eyes see also *Tht.* 143e.) Two scholia (i.e. marginal notes in manuscripts, probably written in late antiquity) on *Clouds* 146 and 223 say that he was bald, but there is no contemporary authority for this, and it may be an inference from his resemblance to a satyr, as satyrs were often represented as bald.

Nothing more is known of the events of his life till 406, when there occurred what was apparently his only intervention, till his trial, in the public life of Athens. Following a naval victory the Athenian commanders had failed to rescue survivors, and the assembly voted that they should be tried collectively, instead of individually as required by law. Most offices being at that time allocated by lot, Socrates happened to be one of the committee who had the task of preparing business for the assembly, and in that capacity he was the only one to oppose the unconstitutional proposal. (That is the version of events

3. The Pnyx, the meeting-place of the Athenian assembly: a view from the Observatory.

reported at *Apol.* 32b–c and by Xenophon in his *Hellenica* (1.7.14–15), but in his *Memorabilia* Xenophon twice (1.1.18, 4.4.2) gives a different version, in which Socrates was the presiding officer of the assembly during the crucial debate, and 'did not allow them to pass the motion' (which, given that the motion was in fact passed, must be understood to mean 'tried unsuccessfully to prevent the motion being put'[2]).)

On the final defeat of Athens in 404 the democratic constitution was suspended and power passed to a junta of thirty who, nominally appointed to revise the laws, soon instituted a reign of terror in which thousands were killed or driven into exile. This lasted for eight months until the tyranny was overthrown in a violent counter-revolution and the democracy restored. Socrates had friends in both camps. Prominent among the Thirty were his associates Charmides and Critias (both relatives of Plato), both of whom were killed in the fighting which accompanied the overthrow of the tyranny, while among the democrats his friends included the orator Lysias and Chaerephon, both of whom were exiled and active in the resistance to the tyrants. Socrates maintained the apolitical stance which he had adopted under the democracy. He remained in Athens, but when the tyrants attempted to involve him by securing his complicity in the arrest of one Leon of Salamis he refused to co-operate 'but just went home' (*Apol.* 32d, cf. Xen. *Mem.* 4.4.3). There is no hint of political opposition, but the same simple refusal to be involved in illegality and immorality which had motivated his stand on the trial of the naval commanders. There is no evidence as to whether he took any part in the overthrow of the tyranny; the silence of Plato and, even more significantly, Xenophon on the issue suggests that he did not.

Trial and Death

Some time in 400 or very early in 399 an obscure young man named Meletus (*Euthyph.* 2b) brought the following indictment against Socrates:

> Meletus son of Meletus of Pitthos has brought and sworn this charge against Socrates son of Sophroniscus of Alopeke: Socrates is a wrongdoer in not recognizing the gods which the city recognizes, and introducing other new divinities. Further, he is a wrongdoer in corrupting the young. Penalty, death.

Two others were associated in bringing the charge: Lycon, also unknown, and Anytus, a politician prominent in the restored democracy. After a preliminary examination (mentioned at the beginning of Plato's *Euthyphro*) before the magistrate who had charge of religious cases, known as the king, the case came to trial before a jury of 500 citizens in the early spring of 399.

4. Remains of the Royal Stoa or *Stoa Basileios*, the headquarters of the King Archon, who was in charge of religious affairs. Socrates came to this building to be formally charged with impiety.

No record of the trial survives. In the years following various authors wrote what purported to be speeches for the prosecution or the defence; two of the latter, by Plato and Xenophon, survive and none of the former. After speeches and production of witnesses by both sides the jury voted for condemnation or acquittal. According to *Apol.* 36a the vote was for condemnation by a majority of sixty, presumably approximately 280 to 220. Once the verdict was reached each side spoke again to propose the penalty, and the jury had to decide between the two. The prosecution demanded the death penalty, while (according to Plato) Socrates, after having in effect refused to propose a penalty (in *Apol.* 36d–e he proposes that he be awarded free meals for life in the town hall as a public benefactor), was eventually induced to propose the not inconsiderable fine of half a talent, over eight years' wages for a skilled craftsman (38b). The vote was for death, and according to Diogenes Laertius eighty more voted for death than had voted for a guilty verdict, indicating a split of 360 to 140; Socrates' refusal to accept a penalty had evidently alienated a considerable proportion of those who had voted for acquittal in the first place.

Execution normally followed very soon after condemnation, but the trial coincided with the start of an annual embassy to the sacred island of Delos, during which, for reasons of ritual purity, it was unlawful to carry out executions (*Ph.* 58a–c). Hence there was an interval of a month (Xen. *Mem.* 4.8.2) between the trial and the execution of the sentence. Socrates was imprisoned during this period, but his friends had ready access to him (*Crito* 43a), and Plato suggests in *Crito* that he had the opportunity to escape, presumably with the connivance of the authorities, to whom the execution of such a prominent figure may well have been an embarrassment (45e, 52c). If the opportunity was available, he rejected it. The final scene is immortalized in Plato's idealized depiction in *Phaedo*. The method of execution, self-administration of a drink of ground-up hemlock, was less ghastly than the normal alternative, a form of crucifixion, but medical evidence indicates that the effects of the poison were in fact much more harrowing than the gentle and dignified end which Plato depicts. According to Plato his last words were 'Crito, we owe a cock to Asclepius; pay it and don't forget' (*Ph.* 118a). Asclepius was the god of health, and the sacrifice of a cock a normal thank-offering for recovery from illness. Perhaps those were in fact his last words, in which case it is interesting that his final concern should have been for a matter of religious ritual. (This was an embarrassment to rationalistic admirers of Socrates in the eighteenth and nineteenth centuries.) But the idealized quality of Plato's description makes it plausible that the choice of these words was determined rather by dramatic appropriateness than by historical accuracy. On that assumption the point may have been to give a final demonstration of Socrates' piety, but that would have been more appropriate to Xenophon's portrayal than Plato's. A recent ingenious suggestion is that the detail refers back to Phaedo's

5. Thought to have contained poison for executions, these small containers were found in a cistern in the state prison.

statement (59b) that Plato was absent from the final scene through illness. The offering is in thanks for Plato's recovery, and marks Plato's succession as Socrates' philosophical heir. This degree of self-advertisement seems implausible; the older view (held by Nietzsche among others) that the thanks is offered on behalf of Socrates himself, in gratitude for his recovery from the sickness of life (cf. Shakespeare's 'After life's fitful fever he sleeps well'), seems more likely.

The lack of any record of the trial makes it impossible to reconstruct precisely what Socrates' accusers charged him with. The explicit accusations cited above are sufficiently vague to allow a wide variety of conduct to fall under them, and in addition Athenian legal practice sanctioned the introduction of material which, while strictly irrelevant to the letter of the charges, might be expected to influence the jury for or against the defendant. An ancient tradition holds that the real ground for the condemnation of Socrates was political, namely, his supposed influence on those of his associates who had become notorious for anti-Athenian and anti-democratic conduct, above all Alcibiades and Critias; thus the orator Aeschines asserted categorically that 'You, Athenians, killed the sophist Socrates because he was seen as having educated Critias, one of the thirty who overthrew the democracy' (*Against Timarchus* 173 (delivered in 345 BC); cf. Xen. *Mem.* 1.2.12–16). Given the notoriety of Alcibiades, Critias, Charmides, and other known associates of Socrates such as Phaedrus and Eryximachus, both of whom had been involved (along with others of the Socratic circle) in a celebrated religious scandal in 415 BC, it would have been very odd had the prosecution not brought up their misdeeds to defame Socrates as a corrupter of the young. An amnesty passed in 403 did indeed prevent people from being charged with crimes committed previously, but that was no bar to citing earlier events as indicative of the defendant's character. It seems, then, virtually certain that the charge of corrupting the young had at least a political dimension. It would not follow that the specifically religious charges were a mere cover for a purely political prosecution, or that the alleged corruption did not itself have a religious as well as a political aspect. We have seen that in the 420s Aristophanes had made Socrates a subverter of traditional religion, whose gods are displaced in favour of 'new divinities' such as Air and Swirl, and a corrupter of sound morality and decent education. It is clear from his *Apology* that Plato thought that some of this mud still stuck in 399, and I see no reason to doubt that he was right. Though the evidence of a whole series of prosecutions of free-thinking intellectuals, including Protagoras and Euripides, in the late fifth century is gravely suspect, it is likely that Anaxagoras was driven from Athens by the threat of prosecution for his impious declaration that the sun was a red-hot stone, and the care which Plato takes in the *Apology* to distance Socrates from Anaxagoras (27d-e) indicates that he saw that case as looming large in the attack on Socrates.

There is also some evidence that Socrates' personal religious behaviour

6. The Death of Socrates. *Crito Closing the Eyes of the Dead Socrates* (1787–92) by Antonio Canova.

and attitudes were seen as eccentric. He famously claimed to be guided by a private divine sign, an inner voice which warned him against doing things which would have been harmful to him, such as engaging in politics (*Apol.* 31c–d), and in the *Apology* (ibid.) he says that Meletus caricatured this in his indictment. Of course, there was nothing illegal or impious in such a claim in itself, but taken together with other evidence of nonconformity it could be cited to show that Socrates bypassed normal channels in his communication with the divine, as Euthyphro suggests in the dialogue (*Euthyph.* 3b, cf. Xen. *Mem.* 1.1.2). Moreover, there is evidence from the fourth century that the Athenian state, while ready enough to welcome foreign deities such as Bendis and Asclepius to official cult status, regarded the introduction of private cults as sufficiently dangerous to merit the death penalty. So any evidence that Socrates was seen as the leader of a private cult would indicate potentially very damaging prejudice against him. We have some hints of such evidence. In *Clouds* Socrates introduces Strepsiades to his 'Thinkery' in a parody of the ceremonies of initiation into religious mysteries (250–74), while a chorus of Aristophanes' *Birds* (produced in 414) describes Socrates as engaged in raising ghosts by a mysterious lake, and his associate Chaerephon, 'the bat' (one of the students of *Clouds*), as one of the ghosts whom he summons (1553–64). We have here the suggestion that Socrates is the leader of a coterie dabbling in the occult, and the episode of his trance at Potidaea, where he stood motionless and lost in thought for twenty-four hours (*Symp.* 220c–d) may have contributed to a reputation for uncanniness. While it may seem to us that the picture of Socrates as an atheistic natural philosopher fits ill with that of a spirit-summoning fakir, that dichotomy may not have seemed so apparent in the fifth century BC; and in any case we are concerned with a climate of thought rather than a precisely articulated set of charges. Socrates, I suggest, was seen as a religious deviant and a subverter of traditional religion and morality, whose corrupting influence had been spectacularly manifested by the flagrant crimes of some of his closest associates.

So much for the case for the prosecution. As for the defence, though there was a tradition (which appears to go back to the fourth century BC) that Socrates offered none at all, the weight of the evidence suggests that he did indeed offer a defence, but one which was by ordinary standards so unusual as to give rise to the belief that he had not prepared it in advance, and/or that he did not seriously expect or even intend it to convince the jury (both in Xen. *Apol.* 1–8). (In all probability the story told by Cicero (*De oratore* 1.231) and others that Lysias wrote a speech for the defence which Socrates refused to deliver as out of character indicates merely that a defence of Socrates was among the speeches attributed to Lysias; see [Plutarch] *Life of Lysias* 836b.) It is natural to enquire how much of the substance of his defence can be reconstructed from the two versions which we possess, those by Plato and Xenophon. The two are very different in character. Plato's, which is over four times as long, purports to be the verbatim text of three speeches delivered by Socrates, the first in reply to the charges, the second, delivered after his conviction, addressed to the question of penalty, and a final address to the jury after their vote for the death penalty. Xenophon's is a narrative, beginning with an explanation of Socrates' reasons for not preparing his defence in advance, continuing with some purported excerpts (in direct speech) from the main defence and the final address to the jury, and concluding with some reports of things which Socrates said after the trial. There are also considerable differences in content. Both represent Socrates as replying in the main speech to the three counts of the indictment, but the substance of the replies is quite different. Xenophon's Socrates rebuts the charge of not recognizing the gods of the city by claiming that he has been assiduous in public worship; he takes the charge of introducing new divinities to refer only to his divine sign, and replies by pointing out that reliance on signs, oracles, etc. is an established element in conventional religion. The charge of corruption is rebutted primarily by appeal to his acknowledged practice of the conventional virtues, backed up by his claim (admitted by Meletus) that what is actually complained of is the education of the young, which should rather be counted benefit than harm. The tone throughout is thoroughly conventional, to such an extent that the reader might well be puzzled why the charges had been brought at all.

Plato's Socrates, by contrast, begins by claiming that the present accusation is the culmination of a process of misrepresentation which he traces back to Aristophanes' caricature, in which the two cardinal falsehoods are (i) that he claims to be an expert in natural philosophy and (ii) that he teaches for pay. (In rebutting the second point he contradicts Xenophon's Socrates in denying that he educates anyone.) In response to the imagined question of what in his actual conduct had given rise to this misrepresentation he does indeed claim that it is possession of a certain kind of wisdom. The explanation of what this wisdom is takes him far beyond Xenophon's Socrates, since it involves nothing less than a defence of his whole way of life as a divine mission, but one of a wholly unconventional kind.

This mission was, according to Plato's Socrates, prompted by a question put by his friend Chaerephon to the oracle of Apollo at Delphi. Chaerephon asked whether anyone was wiser than Socrates, to which the oracle replied that no one was. Since Socrates knew that he possessed no expertise of any sort, he was puzzled what the oracle could mean, and therefore sought to find someone wiser than himself among acknowledged experts (first of all experts in public affairs, subsequently poets and craftsmen). On questioning them about their expertise, however, he found that they in fact lacked the wisdom which they claimed, and were thus less wise than Socrates, who was at least aware of his own ignorance. He thus came to see that the wisdom which the oracle had ascribed to him consisted precisely in this awareness of his ignorance, and that he had a divine mission to show others that their own claims to substantive wisdom were unfounded. This enterprise of examining others (normally referred to as 'the Socratic elenchus', from the Greek *elenchos*, 'examination'), which was the basis of his unpopularity and consequent misrepresentation, he later in the speech describes as the greatest benefit that has ever been conferred on the city, and his obligation to continue it in obedience to the god as so stringent that he would not be prepared to abandon it even if he could save his life by doing so.

This story poses a number of questions, of which the first, obviously, concerns the authenticity of the oracle. Is the story true, or, as some scholars have suggested, is it merely Plato's invention? There are no official records of the Delphic oracle against which we can check the story; the great majority of the oracular responses which we know of are mentioned in literary sources whose reliability has to be considered case by case. The fact that Xenophon too mentions the oracle is no independent evidence, since it is quite likely that he wrote his *Apology* with knowledge of Plato's, and it is therefore possible that he took the story over from him. Certainty is impossible, but my own inclination is to think that the story is true; if it were not, why should Plato identify Chaerephon as the questioner, rather than just 'someone', and add the circumstantial detail that, though Chaerephon himself was dead by the time of the trial, his brother was still alive to testify to the truth of the story? More significant than the historicity of the story is the different use which Plato and Xenophon make of it. According to Xenophon what the oracle said was that no one was more free-spirited or more just or more self-controlled than Socrates, and the story then introduces a catalogue of instances of these virtues on his part, in which wisdom is mentioned only incidentally. According to Plato what the oracle said was that no one was wiser than Socrates, and Socratic wisdom is identified with self-knowledge. Xenophon uses the story to support his conventional picture of Socrates' moral virtue, Plato to present Socratic cross-examination as the fulfilment of a divine mission and therefore as a supreme act of piety.

Another striking feature of Plato's version of the oracle story is the transformation of Socrates' quest from the search for the meaning of the oracle to the lifelong mission to care for the souls of his fellow-citizens by submitting them to his examination. By 23a the meaning of the oracle has been elucidated: 'In reality god [i.e. god alone] is wise, and human wisdom is worth little or nothing . . . He is the wisest among you, o humans, who like Socrates has come to know that in reality he is worth nothing with respect to wisdom.' But this discovery, far from putting an end to Socrates' quest, makes him determined to continue it: 'for this reason I go about to this very day in accordance with the wishes of the god seeking out any citizen or foreigner I think to be wise; and when he seems to me not to be so, I help the god by showing him that he is not wise.' Why is Socrates 'helping the god' by showing people that their conceit of wisdom is baseless? The god wants him to reveal to people their lack of genuine wisdom, which belongs to god alone; but why? It was traditional wisdom that humans should acknowledge their inferiority to the gods; dreadful punishments, such as Apollo's flaying of the satyr Marsyas for challenging him to a music contest, were likely to be visited on those who tried to overstep the gulf. But the benefits accruing from Socratic examination are not of that extrinsic kind. Rather, Socrates' challenge is to 'care for intelligence and truth and the best possible state of one's soul' (29e), since 'it is as a result of goodness that wealth and everything else are good for people in the private and in the public sphere' (30b). There is, then, an intimate relation between self-knowledge and having one's soul in the best possible state; either self-knowledge is identical with that state, or it is a condition of it, necessary, sufficient, or perhaps necessary and sufficient. That is why no greater good has ever befallen the city than Socrates' service to the god.

The details of the relation between self-knowledge and the best state of the soul are not spelled out in the *Apology*. What is clear is that here Plato enunciates the theme of the relation between knowledge and goodness which is central to many of the dialogues, and that that theme is presented in the *Apology* as the core of Socrates' answer to the charge of not recognizing the gods of the city. Unlike Xenophon,

Plato says nothing about Socrates' practice of conventional religious observance, public or private. Instead he presents the philosophic life itself as a higher kind of religious practice, lived in obedience to a god who wants us to make our souls, that is, our selves, as perfect as possible. Each author has Socrates reply to the charge in the terms of his own agenda, Xenophon's of stressing Socrates' conventional piety and virtue, Plato's of presenting him as the exemplar of the philosophic life.

Plato's version of the replies to the other charges shows the power of Socratic questioning. The charge of introducing new divinities is rebutted by inducing Meletus to acknowledge under cross-examination that his position is inconsistent, since he maintains both that Socrates introduces new divinities and that he acknowledges no gods at all, while the charge of corruption is met by the argument that if Socrates corrupted his associates it must have been unintentionally, since if they were corrupted they would be harmful to him, and no one harms himself intentionally. As the latter thesis is central to the ethical theses which Socrates argues for in several Platonic dialogues, we see Plato shaping his reply to the charges against Socrates by reliance, not merely on Socrates' argumentative technique, but also on Socratic ethical theory. Plato sees the accusation of Socrates as an attack, not just on the individual, but, more significantly, on the Socratic practice of philosophy, which is to be rebutted by showing its true nature as service to god and by deploying its argumentative and doctrinal resources. Xenophon's reply, by contrast, has little if any philosophical content.

It is clear, then, that the hope of reconstructing Socrates' actual defence speeches at the trial by piecing together the evidence of our two sources is a vain one, since each of the two presents the defence in a form determined by his own particular agenda. The question of whether any particular statement or argument reported by either Plato or Xenophon was actually made or used by Socrates seems to me unanswerable. Looked at in a wider perspective, it seems to me that Plato's version may well capture the atmosphere of the trial and of Socrates' defence more authentically than Xenophon's, for two reasons. First, the prominence which Plato gives to Aristophanes' caricature and its effects (entirely absent from Xenophon's version) sets the accusation in its historical background and gives much more point to the accusations of religious nonconformity and innovation than does Xenophon. Secondly, the presentation of Socrates' elenctic mission as service to the god and benefit to the city expresses much better than Xenophon's bland presentation the unconventional character of Socrates' defence, and, ironically enough, displays much more forcefully than his own version the arrogance which he says all writers have remarked on and which he sets out to explain.

Chapter 3
Socratic Literature and the Socratic Problem

The account of Socrates' life and death attempted in the previous chapter has already involved us in grappling with the so-called 'Socratic problem', that is, the question of what access our sources give us to the life and character of the historical Socrates. Every statement in that chapter has involved some assumptions, explicit or implicit, about the character and reliability of the source on which it relies. In particular, the account of Socrates' trial emphasizes the different apologetic stances which shape the presentations of Socrates' defence by Plato and Xenophon, concluding that, while we can identify with some plausibility the main lines of the attack on Socrates, our sources merely suggest to us the general tenor of his defence, while leaving us agnostic about the detail. It is the task of this chapter to put that result into context by giving a brief sketch of the extant ancient literature dealing with Socrates and of the genres to which it belongs.

Authors Other Than Plato

On the first kind of Socratic literature, the depiction of Socrates in fifth-century comedy, I have nothing to add to the previous chapter. It is the only Socratic literature known to have been written before Socrates' death, and its depiction of Socrates cannot have been influenced by Plato. It gives us a contemporary caricature, which associates Socrates with some important aspects of contemporary intellectual life, and which we have every reason to believe contributed substantially to the climate of suspicion and hostility which led eventually to his death.

In the opening chapter of his *Poetics* Aristotle refers to 'Socratic conversations' (*Sōkratikoi logoi*) as belonging to an as yet nameless genre of representation together with the mimes of Sophron and Xenarchus, two fifth-century Sicilian writers (apparently father and son). The 'mimes' were dramatic representations of scenes from everyday life (we have a few titles such as *Mother-in-Law* and *The Tuna Fishers*), fictional and apparently comic, classified into those with male and those with female characters; there is no suggestion that the characters portrayed included actual historical individuals. Though Aristotle counts them as belonging to the same genre as Socratic conversations, and Plato was said to have introduced them to Athens and to have been influenced by them in his depictions of character, we should not exaggerate the degree of resemblance, which consists essentially in the fact that both are representations in prose of conversations from (roughly) contemporary life. In particular, we should not jump to the conclusion that because the mimes are wholly fictional, and because Socratic conversations belong to the same genre as the mimes, therefore Socratic conversations are wholly fictional. There is at least one respect in which they are not wholly fictional, in that their characters are mostly taken from real life. The extent to which the depiction of those characters is fictional is a further question.

Ancient sources credit different authors with the invention of the 'Socratic conversation', but there is no dispute that the composition of such conversations was widespread among Socrates' associates, at least nine of whom, in addition to Plato and Xenophon, are mentioned by one source or another as having written them. There is no good evidence that any of this literature was written before Socrates' death, and it is reasonable to assume that its authors shared the intention, explicit in Xenophon, to commemorate Socrates and to defend his memory both against the charges made at the trial and against hostile accounts such as the *Accusation of Socrates*, a pamphlet (now lost) written by a rhetorician named Polycrates some time after 394 BC. Some friends of Socrates are reported by Diogenes Laertius to have made notes of his conversations, and there is no reason to reject that evidence, but just as we must not assume that 'Socratic conversations' were wholly fictional, so we must avoid the opposite error of thinking of them as based on transcripts of actual conversations. The function of note-taking was not to provide a verbatim record for later publication, but to preserve authentically Socratic material for incorporation into broadly imaginative reconstructions.

Apart from the writings of Plato and Xenophon, very little of this literature has survived. For most authors all that we have are titles and occasional snippets. Some of the titles indicate thematic interconnections, including connections with Platonic dialogues. Thus, Crito is said to have written a *Protagoras* and a defence of Socrates; Aeschines, Antisthenes, Eucleides, and Phaedo all wrote an *Alcibiades*; Aeschines and Antisthenes each wrote an *Aspasia* (Aspasia was the celebrated mistress of the statesman Pericles and the inspiration of Plato's *Menexenus*); and Antisthenes wrote a *Menexenus*. A particularly interesting survival is an anonymous papyrus fragment now in Cologne; [3] this contains part of a dialogue between Socrates and an unnamed person in Socrates' cell after his sentence (recalling Plato's *Crito*) in which Socrates is asked why he did not defend himself at the trial. In his answer Socrates is represented as maintaining, as in *Protagoras*, that pleasure is the supreme end of life, a position taken by the Cyrenaic school founded by Socrates' associate Aristippus (also an author of dialogues). It has been plausibly suggested that the author may have belonged to that school. Another possible association with Plato's *Protagoras is* provided by Aeschines' *Callias* (whose house is the setting for Plato's dialogue, as well as for Xenophon's *Symposium*). In addition to his *Alcibiades*, Eucleides of Megara wrote an *Aeschines*, a *Crito*, and an *Eroticus* (the last on a characteristically Socratic theme, as evidenced by Plato's *Phaedrus* and *Symposium* and by Aeschines'

Alcibiades). The prominence of the name of Alcibiades in this catalogue is not accidental. As we saw in the previous chapter, Socrates' association with Alcibiades had certainly fuelled the accusation of corruption of the young and was probably still being used to blacken his reputation after his death; in Xenophon's words (*Mem.* 1.2.12), 'The accuser [perhaps Polycrates] said that Critias and Alcibiades, associates of Socrates, did the greatest harm to the city. For Critias was the most covetous and violent of all the oligarchs, and Alcibiades the most wanton and licentious of all the democrats.' It then became a central theme of Socratic literature to show that, far from encouraging Alcibiades in his wantonness, Socrates had sought to restrain him, and that his crimes (which included sacrilege and treason) had issued from his neglecting Socrates' advice and example, not from following them. Xenophon argues prosaically in *Mem.* 1.2 that (like Critias) he was well behaved as long as he kept company with Socrates and went to the bad only after he ceased to associate with him, and that in any case his motive for associating with Socrates had from the beginning been desire for political power rather than regard for Socrates. (A dangerous argument, for why should desire for power lead him to associate with Socrates, unless he believed that Socrates would help him to attain it?) Plato's depiction in the *Symposium* of Alcibiades' relations with Socrates, presented in the first person by the dramatic character of Alcibiades himself, is intended to make the same point. Socrates' courage and self-control (which withstands the sexual blandishments of the otherwise irresistible Alcibiades) fill him with shame and the recognition that he should do as Socrates bids him, but when he is apart from him he falls under the influence of the flattery of the multitude, so that he would be glad to see Socrates dead (216b–c). The theme of the probably pseudo-Platonic *First Alcibiades* is similar. Alcibiades, convinced that his capacity is greater than that of any of the acknowledged political leaders, is proposing to go into politics, and Socrates' task is to convince him that he is unqualified because he lacks the necessary knowledge, namely, knowledge of what is best. The dialogue ends with Alcibiades promising to be submissive to Socrates,

28

7. A depiction of Alcibiades being reprimanded by Socrates (Italian school, c.1780).

to which Socrates replies, clearly with reference to their respective fates, that he is afraid that the city may prove too strong for them both.

Ambition, shame, and knowledge are similarly central themes in the *Alcibiades* of Aeschines of Sphettus, of which we possess some substantial fragments. Socrates narrates to an unnamed companion a conversation with Alcibiades, beginning by observing how Alcibiades' political ambitions are prompted by emulation of Themistocles, the great statesman who had led Athens in the Persian war of 480. He then points out how Themistocles' achievements were based on knowledge and intelligence, which were yet insufficient to save him from final disgrace and banishment. The point of this is to bring home to Alcibiades his intellectual inferiority to Themistocles and the consequent vanity of his pretensions to rival him, and the strategy is so successful that Alcibiades bursts into tears, lays his head on Socrates' knees, and begs him to educate him. Socrates concludes by telling his companion that he was able to produce this effect not through any skill on his part but by a divine gift, which he identifies with his love for Alcibiades: 'and so although I know no science or skill which I could teach anyone to benefit him, nevertheless I thought that by keeping company with Alcibiades I could make him better through the power of love.' This excerpt combines two themes prominent in Plato's depiction of Socrates: the denial of knowledge or the capacity to teach and the role of love in stimulating relationships whose goal is the education of the beloved (see esp. *Symposium* and *Phaedrus*).

The only other Socratic dialogue of which any substantial excerpts survive (apart from the dialogues of Plato and Xenophon) is Aeschines' *Aspasia*. This also connects with themes in other Socratic writings. It is a dialogue between Socrates and Callias, whose opening recalls Plato's *Apology* 20a–c, but in reverse, since there Socrates reports a conversation in which Callias recommends the sophist Euenus of Paros as a tutor for his sons, whereas in Aeschines' dialogue Callias asks Socrates whom he would recommend as a tutor, and is astonished when Socrates suggests the notorious courtesan Aspasia. Socrates supports his recommendation by instancing two areas in which Aspasia has special expertise: rhetoric, in which she instructed not only the famous Pericles but also Lysicles, another prominent politician; and marriage guidance. The former topic is common to this dialogue and Plato's *Menexenus*, in which Socrates delivers a funeral oration which he says was written by Aspasia who, he adds, had taught rhetoric to many, including Pericles, and had written the famous funeral speech reported by Thucydides in book 2 of his history. The topic of marriage guidance provides an interesting link with Xenophon, for the recipients of Aspasia's wise advice described by Socrates are none other than Xenophon and his wife. (The style of the advice is characteristically Socratic, since Aspasia proceeds by a series of instances in which both husband and wife want to have the best of any kind of thing, dress, horse, etc., to the conclusion that they both want the best spouse, from which she infers that each of them has to make their partnership perfect.) It can hardly be coincidence that Xenophon twice refers to Aspasia's expertise in matchmaking and the training of wives (*Mem.* 2.6.36, *Oec.* 3.14). We should not, of course, suppose that Xenophon had actually benefited personally from Aspasia's expertise, as Aeschines depicts; the point is that this was a common theme in the Socratic literary circle, and that whoever treated it later (a question which the evidence seems to leave open) probably did so with the earlier treatment in mind. We must remain equally agnostic about the relative priority of Plato's *Menexenus* and the *Aspasias* of Aeschines and Antisthenes, and of that of the various *Alcibiadeses*. In general, there seems little if any ground for the attempt to assign relative priority among Socratic works, with the exception of a few cases where Xenophon seems fairly clearly to refer to works of Plato.

The Socratic writings of Xenophon and Plato's Socratic dialogues are the only bodies of Socratic literature to have survived complete. In addition to Xenophon's version of Socrates' defence, we have his *Memorabilia*, four books of reports, mostly in direct speech, of Socrates' conversations; *Symposium*, a lively account of a dinner-party at which Socrates is a guest, similar to and certainly containing references to Plato's *Symposium*; and *Oeconomicus*, a moralizing treatise on estate-management in the form of a Socratic dialogue. The opening of the *Memorabilia* makes it clear that its purpose is primarily apologetic. Xenophon begins by citing the accusation against Socrates and introduces the conversations by elaborating in the first two chapters the themes of his *Apology*, that Socrates was exceptionally pious, of exemplary virtue, and a good influence on his younger associates, some of whom, unfortunately, went to the bad through neglecting his advice. In the rest of the book these themes are developed in a series of conversations, normally between Socrates and one other person, though sometimes it is said that others were present; the interlocutors are mostly familiar figures from the Socratic circle, such as Aristippus, Crito and his son Critobulus, and Xenophon himself, but also including others, such as one of the sons of Pericles, the sophists Antiphon and Hippias, and a high-class prostitute named Theodote. The final chapter returns to the theme which opens the *Apology*, that Socrates did not prepare a defence because his divine sign had indicated to him that it was better for him to die then than to decline into senility, concluding with a eulogy of Socrates as the best and happiest of men, who not only excelled in all the virtues but also promoted them in others.

The work is then essentially a fuller, illustrated version of the *Apology*. In keeping with the character of the latter, the content of the conversations is heavily slanted towards piety, moral uplift, and good practical advice. For example Socrates gives an irreligious acquaintance called Aristodemus a little lecture on the providential ordering of the world, pointing out among other things how the eyelashes are designed to screen the eyes from the wind (1.4), and he encourages the hedonist Aristippus to self-control by telling him a story from the sophist Prodicus of how Heracles chose the sober joys of virtue in preference to the meretricious attractions of vice (2.1). He discusses the role of a general with a series of interlocutors (3.1–5), helps a friend in financial difficulties by persuading him to put the womenfolk of his large household to work making clothes (2.7), and gives advice on the importance of physical fitness (3.12) and on table manners (3.14). This is not to say that the work has no philosophical content. We find Socrates using methods of argument familiar from Plato, such as inductive arguments to establish a conclusion from an array of similar cases (e.g. 2.3), frequently derived from the practice of practical crafts, and there are instances of cross-examination with a view to showing that the person examined lacks the appropriate knowledge (notably 3.6 and 4.2, where the examinations of the respective pretensions to political leadership of Glaucon, Plato's elder brother, and of a young associate named Euthydemus, recall the similar examinations of Alcibiades in Aeschines' *Alcibiades* and the pseudo-Platonic *First Alcibiades*). Two chapters, 3.9 and 4.6, are devoted to philosophical topics familiar from the Platonic dialogues; the former begins with discussion of whether courage is a natural gift or acquired by teaching, a specific instance of the question which begins *Meno* and is prominent in *Protagoras*, and in the course of the chapter (sections 4–5) Xenophon reports that Socrates identified wisdom first with self-control and then with justice and the rest of virtue. That too links this chapter with *Meno* and *Protagoras*, in both of which Socrates defends the thesis that virtue is knowledge. In 4.6 the topic is definition; as in several Platonic dialogues Socrates identifies the question 'What is such-and-such?' (e.g. 'What is justice?') as the primary philosophical question, illustrating the general point by the examples of piety (discussed in *Euthyphro*) and courage (discussed in *Laches*). In section 6 he asserts the 'Socratic paradox' familiar from *Meno*, *Gorgias*, and *Protagoras* that no one knows what he should do but fails to do it, and in section 11 he makes the related claim that those who know how to deal properly with danger are courageous and those who make mistakes cowardly, a thesis which Socrates argues for at *Protagoras* 359–60.

We can sum up by saying that while philosophy takes second place in the *Memorabilia* to piety, morality, and practical advice, the philosophy which the work does contain is recognizably common to other Socratic writings, especially those of Plato. This raises the question whether we should treat Xenophon as an independent source for those elements of philosophical doctrine and method, thus strengthening the case for their attribution to the historical Socrates, or whether we should conclude that Xenophon's source is those very Socratic writings, above all Plato's. We have to tread cautiously. There are indeed some indications in Xenophon's writings of dependence on Plato. *Symposium* 8.32 contains a pretty clear reference to the speeches of Pausanias and Phaedrus in Plato's *Symposium*, and it is at least likely that the many earlier writings on the trial of Socrates, whom Xenophon refers to in *Apology* 1, include Plato's *Apology*.[4] There is nothing in the *Memorabilia* which so clearly points to a specific Platonic reference, and we are not justified in concluding that any similarity of subject-matter must be explained by Xenophon's dependence on Plato, rather than influence in the reverse direction, or reliance on a common source, including memory of the historical Socrates. (We have very little information about the dates of composition of the works of either Plato or Xenophon.) On the other hand, Xenophon left Athens two years before Socrates' death and did not return for more than thirty years. The bulk of his Socratic writings were written during this period of exile, in which he was cut off from personal contact with Athens and must therefore have relied on the writings of other Socratics, including Plato, to refresh his memory and deepen his knowledge of Socrates. Since the philosophical overlaps mentioned above could all be explained by Platonic influence, and since we must assume that Xenophon made some use of Plato's writings in his absence from Athens, the most prudent strategy is to acknowledge that the philosophical elements in the *Memorabilia* should not be treated as an independent source for the philosophy of the historical Socrates. Equally, we have no reason to suppose that either Xenophon's portrayal of Socrates' personality or his presentation of the content of his conversations is any more historically authentic than that of any other Socratic writer. He is indeed himself the interlocutor in one conversation (1.3.8–15), and in some other cases he says that he was present (e.g. 1.4, 2.4–5, 4.3), but in most cases he makes no such claim, and in any case the claim to have been present may itself be part of literary convention; he says that he attended the dinner-party depicted in his *Symposium* (*Symp.* 1.1), whose dramatic date is 422, when he was at most eight years old. Some of the conversations are clear instances of types current in Socratic literature, such as discussions with sophists (1.6, 2.1, 4.4) and cross-examinations of ambitious young men (3.1–6, 4.2–3). The presentation of Socrates' conversations in the *Memorabilia* may indeed owe something to memory of actual Socratic conversations, either Xenophon's own or the memory of others, but (*a*) we have no way of identifying which elements in the work have that source, and (*b*) it is clear that any such elements contribute to a work which is shaped by its general apologetic aim and by the literary conventions of the Socratic genre.

I conclude this section by considering another writer who, though not a writer of Socratic dialogues, has been held to be a source of independent information on the historical Socrates, namely Aristotle. (Aristotle did write dialogues, now lost, but there is nothing to suggest that they were Socratic in the sense of representing conversations of Socrates.) Unlike the others whom we have discussed, Aristotle had no personal acquaintance with Socrates, who died fifteen years before Aristotle was born. He joined Plato's Academy as a seventeen-year-old student in 367 and remained there for twenty years until Plato's death in 347. It is assumed that in that period he had personal association with Plato. There are numerous references to Socrates in his works; frequently the context makes it clear that he is referring to the character of Socrates portrayed in some Platonic work, for example, *Politics* $1261^a5–8$, where he refers to Plato's *Republic* by name, saying 'There Socrates says that wives and children and possessions should be held in common'. Sometimes, however, the context indicates that

Aristotle's intention is to refer to the historical Socrates, and it is with regard to some of these passages that we have to consider whether his presentation of Socrates may plausibly be thought to be independent of Plato's portrayal.

The crucial passage *is Metaphysics* 1078^{b}27–32, where Aristotle, discussing the antecedents of Plato's theory of Forms, says the following:

> There are two things which may justly be ascribed to Socrates, inductive arguments and general definitions, for both are concerned with the starting-point of knowledge; Socrates did not, however, separate the universal or the definitions, but they [i.e. *Plato and his followers*] did, calling them the Forms of things.

Since Plato represents Socrates as maintaining the theory of separately existing Forms in several dialogues, notably *Phaedo* and *Republic*, and referring to it as something which is familiar to everyone taking part in the discussion (*Ph.* 76d, *Rep.* 507a–b), the information that Socrates did not in fact separate universals from their instances cannot have been derived from Aristotle's reading of Plato, and the inference is irresistible that its source was oral tradition in the Academy stemming ultimately from Plato himself. We do not have to suppose either that Aristotle was personally intimate with Plato, his senior by over forty years (though he is said to have been a favourite pupil, and he wrote a poem in praise of Plato), or that personal reminiscences of Socrates were a staple topic of discussion in the Academy. All that we need suppose is that some basic facts about the role of Socrates *vis-à-vis* Plato were common knowledge in the school. It would have been astonishing had that not been so, and the scepticism of some modern scholars on this point is altogether unreasonable. How much this tradition included, beyond the fact that Socrates did not separate the Forms, it is impossible to say. I find it plausible that it included the two positive assertions which Aristotle associates with that negative one, namely, that Socrates looked for universal definitions and that he used inductive arguments.

Plato

Socrates appears in every Platonic dialogue except the *Laws*, universally agreed to be Plato's last work. So, strictly speaking, all of Plato's writings, with the exception of the *Laws*, the *Apology* (which is not a dialogue), and the *Letters* (whose authenticity is disputed) are Socratic dialogues. There are, however, considerable variations in the presentation of the figure of Socrates over the corpus as a whole. In two dialogues acknowledged on stylistic grounds to be late works, the *Sophist* and the *Statesman*, Socrates appears only in the introductory conversation which serves to link those two dialogues to one another and to *Theaetetus*, while the role of the principal participant in the main conversation, normally assigned to Socrates, is assigned to a stranger from Elea (i.e. to a representative of the philosophy of Parmenides). The same situation occurs in two other late dialogues, *Timaeus* and its unfinished sequel *Critias*; in each case Socrates figures briefly in the introductory conversation and the main speaker is the person who gives his name to the dialogue. In *Parmenides* Socrates appears, uniquely, as a very young man, whose main role is to be given instruction in philosophical method by the elderly Parmenides. Even the dialogues where Socrates is the main speaker exhibit considerable variation in portrayal. Some give prominence to events in Socrates' life, notably *Symposium* and those works centred on his trial and death (*Euthyphro, Apology*, *Crito*, and *Phaedo*), but also (to a lesser extent) *Charmides*. Some, including those just mentioned, contain lively depictions of the personality of Socrates and of argumentative interchanges between him and others, with particular prominence given to sophists and their associates. In this group, besides those just mentioned, fall *Protagoras*, *Gorgias*, *Euthydemus*, *Meno*, *Republic* 1, *Hippias Major*, *Hippias Minor*, *Ion*, *Laches*, and *Lysis*. In others again, though Socrates is the principal figure in the sense of directing the course of the discussion, he is much less of an individual personality, and more of a representative figure of philosophical authority, replacable, for all the difference it would make to the course of the discussion, by another; for example, the Eleatic Stranger (or, perhaps, Plato). Such seems to me (though this is a matter for individual judgement) the role of Socrates in *Republic* (except book 1), *Phaedrus*, *Cratylus*, *Theaetetus*, and *Philebus*. How is this plasticity in Plato's portrayal of Socrates to be accounted for, and what are its implications for the relation between that portrayal and the historical Socrates?

In the nineteenth century investigations of stylistic features of the dialogues by various scholars converged independently on the identification of six dialogues: *Sophist*, *Statesman*, *Philebus*, *Timaeus*, *Critias*, and *Laws*, as the latest works in the corpus, identified as such by resemblance in respect of various stylistic features to the *Laws*, which is attested by ancient sources to have been unfinished at Plato's death. This research also identified a further group of four dialogues: *Parmenides*, *Phaedrus*, *Republic*, and *Theaetetus*, as closer than other dialogues to the style of the late group, leading to the hypothesis that these constituted a middle group, written before the late group and after the others. Subsequent stylometric research, while confirming the division into three groups, has not succeeded in establishing any agreed order of composition within any group.[5] This discussion assumes the validity of these results.

For our purpose the most significant feature is the virtual disappearance of Socrates from the late group; he is absent from the *Laws* and from the main discussions of all the others except *Philebus*. His role in that dialogue is similar to that in the dialogues of the middle group with the exception of the anomalous *Parmenides*, where he is assigned the role of interlocutor to Parmenides. In *Philebus*, *Phaedrus*, *Republic*, and *Theaetetus*, though he has the leading role, it is rather as a mouthpiece for philosophical theory and an exponent of argumentative technique than as an individual in debate with other individuals. These distinctions are, of course, matters not only of judgement but also of degree. This is not to suggest that the figure of Socrates in the middle dialogues has no individual traits, or to deny that some of these link him with the figure portrayed in the early dialogues; thus, Socrates in the *Phaedrus* goes barefoot (229a) and hears his divine voice warning him against breaking off the discussion prematurely (242b–c). Moreover, even in the early dialogues the figure of Socrates has a representative role, that of the true philosopher. But what is quite clear is that Plato's interest in the personality of Socrates as the ideal embodiment of philosophy changes in the course of his career as a writer. At the outset that personality is paramount, but gradually its importance declines, and the figure of Socrates comes to assume the depersonalized role of spokesman for Plato's philosophy, to the point where it is superseded by avowedly impersonal figures such as the Eleatic Stranger and the Athenian of the *Laws*. What follows will be concerned primarily with the depiction of Socrates in the dialogues of the early period.

That depiction, it must be re-emphasized, belongs to the genre of 'Socratic conversations', and our earlier warnings against the assumption of naive historicism apply to it as much as they do to the writings of Xenophon and the other Socratics. Unlike Xenophon, Plato never claims to have been present at any conversation which he depicts. He does indicate that he was present at Socrates' trial (*Apol.* 34a, 38b), which I take to be the truth, but we saw that that did not justify taking the *Apology* as a transcript of Socrates' actual speech. In one significant case he says explicitly that he was not present; when at the beginning of the *Phaedo* Phaedo tells Echecrates the names of those who were with Socrates on his last day he adds 'Plato I think was ill' (59b). The effect of this is to distance Plato from the narrative; the eye-witness is not the author himself, but one of his characters, Phaedo, hence that eye-witness's claims are to be interpreted as part of the dramatic context. It follows that what is narrated, for example, that Socrates argued for the immortality of the soul from the theories of Forms and of Recollection, is part of the dramatic fiction. I am inclined to think that Plato's claim to have been absent from Socrates' final scene is as much a matter of literary convention as Xenophon's claims to have been present at Socratic conversations, and that in all probability Plato was actually present.

In some cases (*Charmides*, *Protagoras*) the conversation is represented as having taken place before Plato was born, and in others (*Euthyphro*, *Crito*, *Symposium*) the *mise-en-scène* precludes his presence. Mostly the dialogues contain no claim that they are records of actual conversations, and where that claim is made in particular cases, as in the *Symposium* (172a–174a), the claim is itself part of an elaborate fiction, in which the narrator explains how he is able to describe a conversation at which he was not himself present. The central point is that, for Plato's apologetic and philosophical purposes, historical truth was almost entirely irrelevant; for instance, the main point of the dialogues in which Socrates confronts sophists is to bring out the contrast between his genuine philosophizing and their counterfeit, and in so doing to manifest the injustice of the calumny which, by associating him with the sophists, had brought about his death. For that purpose it was entirely indifferent whether Socrates ever actually met Protagoras or Thrasymachus, or, if he did, whether the conversations actually were on the lines of those represented in *Protagoras* and *Republic* 1. As with Xenophon, it may be that Plato makes some use of actual reminiscence; but we cannot tell where, and it does not in any case matter.

So far we have considered as a single group all those dialogues which stylometric criteria indicate as earlier than the 'middle group': *Parmenides*, *Phaedrus*, *Republic*, and *Theaetetus*. Within that group any differentiation has to appeal to non-stylometric criteria. Here Aristotle's evidence is crucial. Accepting as historical his assertion that Socrates did not separate the Forms, we can identify those dialogues from the stylistically early group in which Socrates maintains the theory of Forms, viz. *Phaedo*, *Symposium*, and *Cratylus*, as dialogues where, in that respect at least, the Socrates of the dialogue is not the historical Socrates. This result can now be supplemented by some conjectures about the likely course of Plato's philosophical development which have at least reasonable plausibility.

It is reasonable to see in the attribution of the theory of Forms to Socrates a stage in the process of the transformation of Socrates into an authoritative figure who speaks more directly for Plato than does the Socrates of his earlier writings. This is indicated by some other features of these dialogues. The *Symposium* puts a good deal of emphasis on the individual personality of Socrates, starting with his unusually smart turn-out for the dinner-party (174a) and his late arrival as a result of having stopped on the way to think out a problem (174d–175b, a mini-version of the trance at Potidaea referred to later in the dialogue (220c–d)), and culminating with Alcibiades' eulogy, which puts it squarely in the Socratic 'Alcibiades dialogue' tradition. But Socrates has another role in the dialogue, that of a spokesman who reports the speech of a wise woman, Diotima, to whom belongs the account of the educational role of love, culminating in the vision of the Form of Beauty (201d–212c). So, strictly, Socrates does not himself maintain the theory, but speaks on behalf of someone else who does. I think that Plato uses this device to mark the transition from the Socrates of historical fact and of the tradition of the Socratic genre (not explicitly distinguished from one another) to what we might call the Platonic Socrates. Socrates speaking with the words of Diotima is a half-way stage to the Socrates *of Phaedo* and *Republic*, who has now incorporated the theory of Forms as his own. As regards *Phaedo*, we saw that Socrates' death depicted there was not his actual death, and it was suggested that Plato has signalled that the narrative does not reproduce what Socrates actually said. Another indication of this is the concluding myth of the fate of the soul after death, where Socrates steps out of his own person to tell what 'is said thus' (107d). The subject matter of *Cratylus*, in particular its interest in linguistic meaning and Heraclitean theories of flux, links it firmly to *Theaetetus* and *Sophist*, to which it can plausibly be seen as a prelude.

Besides the theory of Forms, two other doctrines which it is reasonable to ascribe to Plato are those of the tripartite soul, which does not appear earlier than the middle period *Republic* and *Phaedrus*, and the theory of Recollection, which is plausibly ascribed to Pythagorean influences encountered on his first visit to Sicily in 387 and which is closely linked to the theory of Forms, explicitly in *Phaedo* and *Phaedrus* and, arguably, implicitly in *Meno*. Also closely linked to recollection is the theory of Reincarnation, which is the central topic of the great myths of the afterlife which conclude *Phaedo* and *Republic*, is indicated, though not particularly prominently, in the myth in *Gorgias*, is prominent in the myth in *Phaedrus*, and occurs in some of the arguments of *Meno* and *Phaedo*. My suggestion is that the Socrates who maintains these doctrines is a figure through whom Plato speaks, to a steadily increasing degree, his own words in the voice of Socrates.

This leaves us with a group of stylistically early dialogues in which Socrates does not maintain any of the doctrines which I have identified as specifically Platonic: the theory of Forms, the tripartite account of the soul, recollection, and reincarnation. Leaving out of account the two *Alcibiades* dialogues as probably spurious, and *Menexenus* on account of the fact that it is in essence not a Socratic dialogue but a parody of a funeral oration, these are: *Apology, Euthyphro, Crito, Charmides, Laches, Lysis, Ion, Euthydemus, Protagoras*, and the two *Hippias* dialogues (of which the authenticity of *Hippias Major is* also disputed). To these should be added *Gorgias* and *Meno* as, probably, transitional works containing features linking them both to the early group and to the middle 'Platonic' dialogues. This is not to say that the Socrates of these dialogues is the historical Socrates. Plato, like every other Socratic writer, has from the outset concerns to which historical truth is incidental; in Plato's case these are the defence of Socrates and the presentation of Socratic argument as a paradigm of philosophy.

These dialogues do, however, present a picture of Socrates which is coherent both psychologically and (to a reasonable extent, though not wholly) doctrinally. Moreover, that picture is closer to the historical reality to this extent: first, that the kind of discussion which is there presented is probably more like actual Socratic conversations than the more technical argumentation of, say, *Theaetetus*, and secondly, that the Socrates in these dialogues carries a lighter burden of Platonic doctrine.

As far as Plato's portrayal of Socrates is concerned, there is no sharp line to be drawn between 'the historical Socrates' and 'the Platonic Socrates'. The Platonic Socrates is simply Plato's presentation of Socrates in his writings. That presentation, as I hope the foregoing sketch has indicated, undergoes an intelligible development from the portrayal of a highly individual personality engaged in a highly characteristic kind of philosophical activity to the mere ascription of the label 'Socrates' to the lay figure which represents Plato's opinions. The earliest stage of that process, though closer to historical reality, is never a simple depiction of it, and the transition from that stage to a more 'Platonic' stage is continuous, not a sharp cut-off.

The next chapter examines the content of that early stage of the presentation of Socrates. Two presuppositions of this discussion should be made explicit. The first is that, while critical examination of the views of others is Socrates' principal method of enquiry, the aim of that method is at least sometimes to provide arguments in support of certain theses which Socrates maintains, not merely to reveal inconsistency among the beliefs of those to whom he is talking.[6] The second is that the dialogues should not be read in isolation from one another. Some contemporary scholars, reviving the view maintained in the nineteenth century by Grote, suggest that there should be no greater expectation of consistency of doctrine or of the pursuit of common themes in the Platonic dialogues than in the corpus of a dramatist such as Sophocles. I believe, on the contrary, that Plato throughout portrays Socrates engaged as a philosopher in the search for truth and understanding, and that the individual works which make up that portrayal may therefore be expected to give a coherent picture of his philosophical activity. That is not, of course, to deny that Plato can represent Socrates as changing his mind, or to deny that his portrayal of Socrates changes to reflect shifts in his own philosophical standpoint (some such changes are discussed in the next chapter). All that I am maintaining is that Plato presents Socrates as seeking to work out a broadly coherent position, against the background of which changes and developments have to be seen and explained.

Chapter 4
Plato's Socrates

As indicated at the end of the last chapter, we shall be considering the portrayal of Socrates' doctrines and methods of argument in twelve dialogues plus *Apology*. The following features are common to all or most of these dialogues.

i.   *Characterization of Socrates*. Socrates is predominantly characterized, not as a teacher, but as an enquirer. He disclaims wisdom, and seeks, normally in vain, elucidation of problematic questions from his interlocutors, by the method of elenchus, that is, by critically examining their beliefs. In some dialogues, notably *Protagoras* and *Gorgias*, the questioning stance gives way to a more authoritative tone.

ii.   *Definition*. Many of the dialogues are concerned with the attempt to define a virtue or other ethically significant concept. *Euthyphro* asks 'What is holiness or piety?', *Charmides* 'What is temperance?', *Laches* 'What is courage?', *Hippias Major* 'What is fineness or beauty?' Both *Meno*, explicitly, and *Protagoras*, implicitly, consider the general question 'What is virtue or excellence?' In all these dialogues the discussion ends in ostensible failure, with Socrates and his interlocutor(s) acknowledging that they have failed to find the answer to the central question; in some cases there are textual indications of what the correct answer is.

iii.   *Ethics*. All these dialogues are concerned with ethics in the broad sense of how one should live. Besides those dialogues which seek definitions, *Crito* deals with a practical ethical problem: should Socrates try to escape from prison after his sentence; and both *Gorgias* and *Euthydemus* examine what the aims of life should be. The only ostensible exception is *Ion*, which is an examination of the claim of a professional reciter of poetry to possess wisdom. But even that ties in closely with the general ethical interest of these dialogues, since the debunking of Ion's claims to wisdom has the implication that both poets and their interpreters are directed not by wisdom, but by non-rational inspiration, and hence that poetry has no claim to the central educational role which Greek tradition ascribed to it. This little dialogue should be seen as an early essay on the topic which preoccupies much of Plato's writing, namely, the aims of education and the proper qualifications of the educator.

iv. *Sophists*. In several of these dialogues, namely, the *Hippias* dialogues, *Protagoras*, *Gorgias*, *Euthydemus*, and *Meno*, that topic is pursued via the portrayal of a confrontation between Socrates on the one hand and various sophists and/or their pupils and associates on the other. These dialogues thereby develop the apologetic project enunciated in the *Apology*.

These topics will now be considered in more detail.

Socrates' Disavowal of Wisdom

That Socrates denied having any knowledge, except the knowledge that he had no knowledge, became a catchword in antiquity. But that paradoxical formulation is a clear misreading of Plato. Though Socrates frequently says that he does not know the answer to the particular question under discussion, he never says that he knows nothing whatever, and indeed he makes some emphatic claims to knowledge, most notably in the *Apology*, where he twice claims to know that abandoning his divine mission would be bad and disgraceful (29b,

37b). What he does disavow is having any wisdom (*Apol.* 21b), and consequently he denies that he educates people, clearly understanding education as handing on a body of wisdom or learning (19d–20c). Given his assertions in the *Apology* that only god is truly wise and human wisdom is nothing in comparison to that true wisdom (23a–b), the denial of wisdom might be understood as simply the acceptance of human limitations. To possess wisdom would be to have the complete and totally perspicuous understanding of everything which is the prerogative of god. Neither Socrates nor anyone else can hope to aspire to that, and in denying that he has it Socrates is simply setting his face against a human arrogance which is none the less blasphemous for being virtually universal.

But while the devaluation of human wisdom as such is indeed a strain in the *Apology*, in denying that he possesses wisdom and, consequently, that he teaches people, Socrates is contrasting his own condition, not with the divine wisdom, but with a human paradigm of wisdom. This paradigm is realized by craftsmen such as builders and shoemakers who, he acknowledges (22d–e) do possess wisdom in the sense that they are masters of their craft, though they go wrong in thinking that their special expertise extends to matters outside the scope of the craft. This expertise is a structured body of knowledge which is systematically acquired and communicated to others, by possession of which the expert is able reliably to solve the practical problems posed by the craft and to explain the grounds of their solution. The sophists claimed to possess, and to teach to others, such an expertise applying to overall success in social and personal life, the 'political craft' (*politikē technē*) (*Prot.* 319a, *Apol.* 19d–20c). Though Socrates rejects these claims, it is not on the ground that such expertise is not available to human beings, but on the ground that the sophists' activity fails to meet the ordinary criteria for being a genuine expertise, for example, that of being systematically learned and taught (*Prot.* 319d–320b, *Meno* 89c–94e). He denies that he possesses this expertise himself (*Apol.* 20c), but does not say that it is impossible that he, or anyone, could possess it.

There is, then, no ground to assume that Socrates' disavowal of knowledge is an instance of what has become known as 'Socratic irony', that is, pretended ignorance for dialectical purposes. Socrates does indeed frequently pose as admiring the supposedly superior knowledge of the person he is talking to (e.g. *Euthyph.* 5a–b, where he says that he ought to take instruction from Euthyphro on how to defend himself against Meletus' accusation), but the reader, at any rate, is clearly not supposed to be taken in; on the contrary, these avowals serve to point up the particularly controversial character of what the interlocutor has said, or the dubiousness of his claim to authority. The context of the *Apology*, however, rules out any such dialectical function for the disavowal of knowledge. Socrates is not there posing as deferring to a supposed, but actually bogus, epistemic authority; he is with perfect sincerity matching his own epistemic state against an appropriate paradigm, and finding it wanting.

If the disavowal of knowledge is in fact the disavowal of wisdom or expertise, we can see how that disavowal is compatible with the particular claims to knowledge which Socrates makes. The non-expert can know some particular things, but not in the way that the expert knows them; specifically those particular items of knowledge do not fit into a comprehensive web of knowledge which allows the expert to provide explanations of their truth by relating them to other items and/or to the structure as a whole. But how does the non-expert know those things? Usually, by having been told, directly or indirectly, by an expert. Socrates does not, however, recognize any experts, at least human experts, in matters of morality. So how does he know, for example, that he must not abandon his mission to philosophize, whatever the cost? A possible answer is that he has been told this by god, who is an expert in morality. But, leaving aside questions (suggested by *Euthyphro*) of how he knows that god is an expert in morality, that is not in fact an answer which is given or even suggested in *Apology* or elsewhere.

One might attempt to dissolve the problem by suggesting that Socrates does not intend to claim knowledge of these things, but merely to express his beliefs. But Plato makes him say that he knows them, so why should we suppose that Plato does not represent him as meaning what he says? As we have seen, Socrates does indeed recognize an ideal epistemic paradigm which he fails to satisfy, yet he claims knowledge in particular cases. The suggestion being considered amounts to this, that satisfaction of the paradigm is to be equated with knowledge, while the epistemically less satisfactory state which Socrates is in is to be relegated to that of belief. But the distinction between paradigm-satisfying and epistemically inferior states can be maintained without denying the latter the title of knowledge, by using the distinction between the expert's integrated knowledge and the non-expert's fragmentary knowledge. (We might, if we choose, talk of the former as knowledge 'strictly speaking' and the latter as knowledge 'for ordinary purposes' or 'in a loose and popular sense'. Plato does not in fact use such locutions, but the essential distinction is unaltered.) We are, then, still left with the question how Socrates, an avowed non-expert in matters of morality, knows the particular moral truths which he claims to know.

The straightforward, though perhaps disappointing, answer is that Socrates does not say how he knows those truths. Consideration of his argumentative practice may give us some clues. Often his arguments seem intended to do no more than reveal that his interlocutor has inconsistent beliefs about some matter on which he purports to have knowledge, and thereby to undermine that claim to knowledge, as Socrates describes himself in the *Apology* as doing. But at least sometimes he clearly thinks that, provided his interlocutor maintains nothing but what he sincerely believes, the critical examination of those beliefs will reveal, not merely inconsistency among them, but the falsehood of some belief. A particularly clear case is the claim of Polus and Callicles in *Gorgias* that it is better to do wrong than to suffer it. Socrates claims (479e) that the critical arguments by which he has led Polus to accept the contrary thesis that it is worse to do wrong than to suffer it have proved that the latter is true, and asserts even more emphatically at the end of the argument with Callicles (508e–509a) that that conclusion has been 'tied down with arguments of iron and adamant' (i.e. of irresistible force). Yet this very strong claim is conjoined with a disavowal of knowledge: 'My position is always the same, that I do not know how these things are, but no one I have ever met, as in the present case, has been able to deny them without making himself ridiculous.'

Here we have a contrast between expert knowledge, which Socrates disavows, and a favourable epistemic position produced by repeated application of the elenchus. There are some propositions which repeated experiment shows no one to be capable of denying without self-contradiction. Commitment to these is always in principle provisional, since there is always the theoretical possibility that someone might come up with a new argument which might allow escape even from the 'arguments of iron and adamant', as Socrates acknowledges (509a2–4). But realistically, Socrates clearly believes, the arguments rely on principles which are so firmly entrenched that there is no practical possibility of anyone's denying them. Might the truths which Socrates knows non-expertly be truths which he has thus established via the elenchus? While that is an attractive suggestion, we have to acknowledge that it has no clear textual confirmation. In *Crito* (49a) the fundamental proposition that one must never act unjustly is said to be one which Socrates and Crito have often agreed on, and that agreement is to bind them in considering the propriety of Socrates' attempting to escape from prison. The implication is, surely, that the agreement was based on reasons which are still in force; otherwise why should Socrates and Crito not change their minds? But there is nothing to suggest that those reasons took the form of elenchus of Socrates' and Crito's beliefs.

Our conclusion has to be that, though Socrates treats elenchus of the interlocutor's belief as sometimes revealing truth, and though the achieving of truth by that means provides a possible model for non-expert knowledge, we are not justified in attributing to Socrates the claim that all non-expert moral knowledge is in fact achieved via that method. He gives some indication that he knows some moral truths on the strength of having a good argument for them, but he gives no general account of the conditions for non-expert moral knowledge.

Gorgias is the dialogue which provides the clearest cases in which the elenchus is seen as leading to the discovery of truth, and it is probably not coincidental that in the same dialogue we find Socrates abandoning his stance as a non-expert questioner and claiming expertise. One of the themes of the dialogue is the role of rhetoric in education, that is, in promoting the good life. Socrates sets up a taxonomy of genuine crafts concerned respectively with the good of the soul and that of the body, and of counterfeits corresponding to each (463a–465a). The generic name for the craft concerned with the good of the soul is *politikē*, the art of life, subdivided into legislation, which promotes the good of the soul (as gymnastics promotes the good of the body), and justice, which preserves it (as medicine preserves the good of the body). Rhetoric is the bogus counterpart of *politikē*, since the aim of the orator is not to promote people's good, but to pander to their wishes by enabling them to get what they want through the power of persuasion. It thus promotes, not the genuinely good life, but a spurious appearance of it, as cosmetics is the skill, not of making people actually healthy, but of making them look healthy (465c). *Politikē* is thus a genuine expertise, and in striking contrast to his stance in the *Apology* we find Socrates not merely claiming that he practises it, but that no one else does (521d), since he alone cares for the good of his fellow-citizens.

This conception of Socrates as the only genuine practitioner of *politikē* recurs in an image at the conclusion of *Meno* (99e–100a), where Socrates sums up the conclusion of the argument that goodness cannot be taught, but is acquired by a divine gift without intelligence 'unless there were one of the *politikoi* who was capable of making someone else *politikos*' (i.e. unless there were someone who could pass his expertise in the art of life on to another, as conventional politicians have shown themselves incapable of doing). He goes on to say that such a man would be like Homer's description of Tiresias in the underworld (in the *Odyssey*): 'He alone of those in Hades is alive, and the rest flit about like shadows.' This reference to Odysseus' visit to the underworld in *Odyssey* 11 picks up the description of Socrates' meeting with the sophists in *Protagoras*, where Socrates refers to the sophists by quoting the words of Odysseus (315b–c), thereby casting himself as a living man and the sophists as shadows (i.e. ghosts). He is then the real expert in the art of life 'the real thing with respect to goodness, compared with shadows' (*Meno* 100a), who has (in *Meno* and *Protagoras*) a positive conception of the nature of goodness and (in *Meno*) a new method of transmitting that conception to others. This is the method of recollection, in which knowledge which the soul has possessed from all eternity but forgotten in the process of reincarnation is revived via the process of critical examination.

The development of this more authoritative figure of Socrates is a feature of dialogues which we identified as transitional between the earlier 'Socratic' dialogues and the dialogues of Plato's middle period. It is a particular instance of the gradual metamorphosis of the figure of Socrates into the representative of Plato which we noted earlier.

Definition

Socrates' interest in definitions arises from his quest for expertise. The expert knows about his or her subject, and according to Socrates the primary knowledge concerning any subject is precisely knowledge of what that subject is. The connection with expertise is made explicit in *Hippias Major* (286c–d), where Socrates tells Hippias how, when he was praising some things as fine and condemning others as disgraceful, he was rudely challenged by someone who said, 'How do you know what sorts of thing are fine and what sorts disgraceful? Tell me, could you say what fineness is?' Being unable to meet this challenge he consults Hippias, whose universal expertise includes, as 'a small and unimportant part', knowledge of what fineness is; if Hippias were unable to answer that question his activity would be 'worthless and inexpert' (286e).

The primacy of the 'What is such-and-such?' question is emphasized in a number of dialogues. The general pattern of argument is that some specific question concerning a subject, which is the actual starting-point of discussion, for example, how one is to acquire goodness, is problematic in the absence of an agreed conception of what that subject, in this case goodness, is. Hence, though the specific question is psychologically prior, in that that is where one actually begins the enquiry, the 'What is X?' question is epistemologically prior, in the sense that it is impossible to answer the former without having answered the latter but not vice versa. The problematic question may be of various kinds. In *Laches* (189d–190d) it is how a particular virtue, courage, is to be inculcated, while in *Meno* (70a–71b) and *Protagoras* (329a–d, 360e–361a) it is the generalization of that question to goodness as such. In *Republic* 1 (354b–c) it is whether justice is advantageous to its possessor. In *Euthyphro* (4b–5d) it is whether a particular disputed case, Euthyphro's prosecution of his father for homicide, is or is not an instance of piety or holiness. Similarly, at *Charm*. 158c–59a the question of whether Charmides has self-control is treated as problematic, and therefore as requiring prior consideration of what self-control is.

The pattern exhibited by the last two examples, in which the question 'Is this an instance of property F?' is said to be unsettleable without a prior answer to the question 'What is E?', has given rise to the accusation that Socrates is guilty of what has been dubbed 'the Socratic fallacy', namely, maintaining that it is impossible to tell whether anything is an instance of any property unless one is in possession of a definition of that property. That thesis would be disastrous for Socrates to maintain, not merely because it is open to countless counter-examples (e.g. we can all tell that a five-pound note is an instance of money even if we are unable to give a definition of money), but because Socrates' approved strategy for reaching a definition is to consider what instances of the kind or property in question have in common (e.g. *Meno* 72a–c). Obviously, if we cannot tell which are the instances of the kind or property in question in advance of giving the definition that procedure is futile, as is the procedure of rejecting a definition by producing a counter-example, for if you cannot tell whether any instance is an instance without a definition, equally you cannot tell whether any instance is not an instance without a definition. But since the production of counter-examples is one of the standard procedures of Socratic elenchus, the fallacy would be wholly destructive of Socrates' argumentative method.

In fact, Socrates is not committed to that methodologically self-destructive position. The most that the examples in *Euthyphro* and *Charmides* commit him to is that there are some, disputed, instances, where the question 'Is this an instance of E?' cannot be settled without answering the prior question 'What is E?'. That claim does not commit him to maintaining that there are no undisputed cases, and so leaves it open to him to look for a property present in all the undisputed cases of F and absent from all the undisputed cases of non-F, and then to settle the disputed cases by determining whether that property applies to them. (In fact that procedure is bound to leave the dispute unsettled, because the original dispute is now transformed into a dispute over the propriety of widening the extension of the property from the undisputed to the disputed cases. That, however, is another question.)

54

Socrates' rude challenger in *Hippias Major* does, however, appear to go so far as to claim that it is impossible to tell whether any particular thing is fine before one has given a definition of fineness. When all Socrates' and Hippias' attempts at defining fineness have failed, Socrates imagines himself being confronted again by the challenger and asked, 'How will you know whether any speech has been finely put together, or any action whatever finely done, if you are ignorant of fineness? And if you are in that state, do you think you are better off alive than dead?' (304d–e). We cannot avoid the difficulty by saying simply that this is someone else's view, not Socrates', since Socrates makes it clear that the rude challenger is an alter ego; 'he happens to be very nearly related to me and lives in the same house' (304d). Yet the rude challenger's view is not one which Socrates simply endorses, for he concludes (304e) by saying that he thinks he knows that the proverb 'Fine things are difficult' is true; but on the challenger's account he could not be in a position to know even that. The challenger's view, then, is not after all Socrates' own; it is very closely related to it, indeed (and thereby likely to be confused with it), and constitutes a challenge in that, if accepted, it would overthrow Socrates' entire argumentative methodology. Hence the challenge is to distinguish that view from Socrates' actual, more modest view that there are some difficult cases which cannot be settled without the ability to give a definition. To be an expert in an area is to be able to tell reliably, for disputed and undisputed cases alike, whether any case is an instance of the property or kind in question, and for that, according to Socrates, it is necessary, as well as sufficient, to be able to say what the property or kind is.

The examples from *Laches*, *Meno*, *Protagoras*, and *Republic* 1 exhibit another pattern; here the question which gives rise to the quest for the definition of a property is not whether a given, disputed, instance falls under it, but whether that property itself has some further property, specifically whether justice is beneficial to its possessor, and whether courage and overall goodness (i.e. the possession of all the virtues,

55

courage, self-control, justice, wisdom, etc.) can be taught. At *Meno* 71b Socrates gives an analogy for this pattern of the priority of definition which suggests that it is the most basic platitude. If I don't know at all who Meno is, I can't know whether he has any property, for example, whether he is rich or handsome. Similarly, if I don't know at all what goodness is, there is no possibility of my knowing anything about it, including how it is to be acquired.

Understood in a particular way, this is indeed a platitude. If I have never heard of Meno, the appropriate reply to the question 'Is Meno handsome?' is 'Sorry, I don't know whom you mean.' Similarly, if I have no idea what goodness is, the appropriate reply to 'Can goodness be taught?' is 'Sorry, I don't know what you're talking about.' Here we have cases where a prerequisite of intelligible speech about a subject, that one should be able to identify the subject, is not fulfilled. Clearly, that prerequisite of intelligible speech does not require the ability to give a definition of the subject. In the case of an individual subject such as Meno one does not have to be in possession of any specification of Meno which uniquely specifies him independently of context; one might, for instance, be able to identify him only ostensively as 'That man over there', or indefinitely as 'Someone I met in a pub last year'. The analogue in the case of a universal such as goodness is no more than the minimal requirement to know what we are talking about when we use the word; but that again does not presuppose the ability to give a verbal specification (i.e. a definition) of the universal. To return to our earlier example, I can know what I am talking about when I use the word 'money', even if I am unable to give a definition of money; it is clearly enough that I can, for instance, recognize standard instances. Now, in that sense it is clear that Meno knows what he is talking about from the very start; otherwise he could not even raise his initial question 'Can goodness be taught?' So the platitude that intelligible speech about any subject requires the ability to identify that subject does not point towards the priority of definition. Why, then, does Socrates insist on that priority even though the condition which the platitude specifies is satisfied?

To answer that question we need to observe that in *Laches*, *Meno*, and *Protagoras* the search for the definition of particular virtues and inclusive goodness is prompted by the practical question of how those qualities are to be acquired. What kind of definition of those qualities is demanded by the practical question? Clearly, something more than the bare ability to know what one is talking about is demanded, because, as we have seen, that ability is presupposed by the asking of the practical question itself. It is tempting to suggest that what more is required is just the ability to elucidate the dictionary meaning of the term designating the quality under discussion. In the case of the Greek term which I have rendered distributively as 'virtue' and collectively as 'goodness' (*aretē*), a reasonably accurate specification of its meaning would be:

1. An attribute of an agent, one of a set of attributes severally necessary and jointly sufficient for the attainment of overall success in life.
2. The set of attributes specified under 1.

How is the ability to give that elucidation demanded by the practical question? It does indeed advance the enquiry to the extent of making it clear that the search is for properties which promote success in life, but it gives no indication what properties those are, nor, crucially, how those properties are to be acquired. People could agree on that definition but disagree radically in their answers to the practical question, if, for instance, some thought that the properties which bring success in life are all gifts of nature such as intelligence and noble lineage, while others thought that they could all be acquired through practice like practical abilities. The practical question thus appears to demand a different kind of definition from the elucidation of the meaning of the term which designates the property; it demands a substantive specification of what that property is. A substantive specification will include both the decomposition of a complex of properties into the components of that complex (e.g. goodness consists of justice, self-control, etc.) and explanatory accounts of those properties (e.g. self-control consists in the control of the bodily appetites by reason). That is to say, it provides a theory of goodness, which explains it by identifying its constituents and causes, and thereby indicates appropriate methods of acquiring it.

That the definitions sought are of this substantive kind chimes in well with the demand that the giving of definitions is what characterizes the expert. The expert on goodness should be able to explain what goodness is with a view to providing reliable guidance on how to acquire and maintain goodness, just as the expert on health should be able to explain what health is with a view to providing reliable guidance on how to become and stay healthy. The texts of the dialogues mentioned above provide some confirmation that the definitions sought are of this kind, though it would be an oversimplification to pretend that they are distinguished with total clarity from elucidations of the meanings of the terms designating the properties in question.

That Socrates' search is for substantive rather than purely conceptual or 'analytic' definitions is indicated by those dialogues which either explicitly identify or suggest the identification of goodness with knowledge or some other cognitive state. The most detailed discussion occurs in *Meno* (suggested above to be transitional between 'Socratic' and 'Platonic'). At 75–6 Socrates attempts to explain to Meno that he is looking not for lists of specific virtues such as courage and self-control but for a specification of what those virtues have in common, and illustrates this by giving two model specifications, first of shape and then of colour. Of these, the former is a conceptual elucidation, namely, that shape is the limit of a solid, and the second a 'scientific' account of colour (based on the theory of the fifth-century philosopher

Empedocles) as a stream of particles flowing out from the perceived object, of appropriate size and shape to pass through channels in the eye to the internal perceptive organ. Socrates gives no clear indication that he regards these specifications as of different kinds; he says that he prefers the former, but does not indicate why, except that he describes the latter as 'high-flown', perhaps indicating that it is inferior because it is couched in over-elaborate technical terminology. Despite this expressed preference for what is in fact a conceptual elucidation over a substantive definition, Socrates then goes on to propose an account of goodness of the latter kind, namely, that goodness is knowledge. This is not itself an elucidation of the concept of goodness, as specified above, though it does depend on a conceptual thesis, that goodness is advantageous to its possessor (in Greek, that *aretē* is *ōphelimon*, 87e). Rather, it is the identification of knowledge as that state which is in fact necessary and/or sufficient for success in life, and it is arrived at not purely by considering the meanings of words but by the adducing of a highly general thesis about how success is achieved. The thesis is that since every other desirable property, such as strength or boldness, can lead to disaster, the only unconditionally good thing is that which provides the proper direction of those qualities, namely, intelligence, which is equated with knowledge (87d–89c). Again, Socrates is led ostensibly to abandon that account in favour of the revised suggestion that goodness is not knowledge but true belief (89c–97c) by consideration of the alleged empirical fact that there are no experts in goodness, as there would have to be if goodness were some kind of knowledge (another conceptual thesis). In Socrates' arguments conceptual theses and general empirical claims about human nature mesh to provide the best available theory of what goodness really is, that is, of what property best fits the specification set out in the elucidation of the concept given above.

In *Meno*, then, the practical question of how goodness is acquired leads to a substantive account of goodness as a cognitive state. It is no coincidence that the two other dialogues which begin from that question, either about goodness in general (*Protagoras*) or about a particular virtue (courage in *Laches*), exhibit a similar pattern of development. In *Protagoras* Socrates' young friend Hippocrates begins by assuming that the way to acquire goodness is to be taught it by Protagoras, but the sophist's conception of goodness as a cluster of only contingently connected attributes is rejected in favour of what is in effect a version of the theory proposed in *Meno*, that goodness is knowledge. In *Laches* the question of how courage is to be acquired leads, after the rejection of various alternative suggestions, to a specific version of the theory that goodness is knowledge, namely, that courage is knowledge of what is and what is not to be feared (194e–195a). This is eventually rejected on the grounds that, since what is and what is not to be feared is identical with what is and what is not bad, courage will then just be the knowledge of what is and what is not bad. But since, on this cognitive account, that is precisely what goodness as a whole is, courage will be identical with goodness as a whole, instead of a part of it, as was the original hypothesis (198a–199e). Hence the dialogue ends with the admission that the participants have failed in their search for what courage is. Commentators disagree on whether this inconclusive outcome is to be taken at face value, and, if not, which of the assumptions which lead to it should be abandoned. The significant point to observe is that here again the practical question leads not merely to a substantive account of the property in question but towards the same account as is canvassed in *Meno* and *Protagoras*.

I do not wish to suggest that at the time of writing these dialogues Plato had a clear grasp of the distinction between purely conceptual definitions and the substantive type of account exemplified by the cognitive theory. The fact that even in the dialogue which discusses definition in greatest detail, *Meno*, which I assume to have been one of the latest of the dialogues I discuss, he gives as model definitions an example of either kind without any explicit differentiation suggests that he had not arrived at any theoretical discrimination between the two. My suggestion is rather that his practice shows him favouring a kind of definition which we can characterize as substantive rather than conceptual, and that the practical orientation of the discussions leading to those definitions provides an explanation of that fact.

Sometimes the course of the dialogue is even less clearly indicated. In *Euthyphro* the initial question is 'What property is it in virtue of which things (especially kinds of actions) are holy?' When Euthyphro suggests (6e–7a) that it is the property of being approved of by the gods (which is very close to an elucidation of the ordinary Greek conception of *to hosion*), Socrates elicits from him the assertion that the gods approve of holy things *because they are holy* (10d). This excludes the possibility that holiness should be that very property of being approved of by the gods, and points the rest of the discussion in the direction of a search for the kind of conduct which attracts the gods' approval. Here too we may say that Socrates is groping towards a substantive account of holiness, in that the answer would have to be given in terms of a theory of human nature and its relation to the divine, but the dialogue provides no more than hints as to the detailed form of such a theory. The situation in *Charmides* is even less clear-cut, partly because the virtue under discussion, *sōphrosunē* (conventionally translated 'self-control', but sometimes better rendered 'soundness of mind'), is genuinely indeterminate between a style of behaviour and the mental and motivational state directing it. Hence the various suggestions that it is one kind or another of knowledge are less easy to classify as either conceptual elucidations or substantive accounts than the suggested definitions in *Laches*, *Meno*, and *Protagoras*.

Ethics

The search for definitions, then, is the search for expertise, and the possessor of expertise possesses a theory of the subject-matter of that expertise, a grasp of its nature which delivers answers to further questions, both theoretical and practical, about it. In the dialogues discussed in the previous section we see Socrates searching for such a theory applied to human goodness, in some cases a theory of one of the constituents of goodness, that is, an individual virtue (piety in *Euthyphro*, courage in *Laches*, and self-control in *Charmides*), in others (*Meno*, *Protagoras*) a theory of goodness as a whole. In all of these the search is, at least ostensibly, unsuccessful, in that each dialogue ends with the acknowledgement by Socrates and his interlocutors that they have not arrived at the account of goodness or of its parts which they were seeking. But there are some discernible differences. In the three dialogues dealing with individual virtues the discussion is more tentative, Socrates is not readily identified with any positive position, and it is at least plausible to accept the final impasse at its face value. In *Meno* and *Protagoras*, on the other hand, Socrates argues firmly for the thesis that virtue is knowledge, and it is plausible to think that the ostensibly aporetic conclusions are to be interpreted as not detracting from his commitment to that thesis. In these dialogues, it seems to me, Plato depicts Socrates not indeed as possessing the fully developed theory of goodness which is his goal but at least as having a grasp of its general shape. There is, then, even within the dialogues of definition, a development in the portrayal of Socrates from that of purely critical searcher to the proponent of theory (though not expert in the fullest sense). It is an open question whether this development is one within Plato's perception of the historical Socrates, or the first stage of a development from that perception to a presentation containing more of his own views.

The basis of the theory is the combination of the conception of goodness as that property which guarantees overall success in life with the substantive thesis that what in fact guarantees that success is knowledge of what is best for the agent. This in turn rests on a single comprehensive theory of human motivation, namely, that the agent's conception of what is overall best for him- or herself (i.e. what best promotes *eudaimonia*, overall success in life) is sufficient to motivate action with a view to its own realization. This motivation involves desire as well as belief; Socrates maintains (*Meno* 77c, 78b) that everyone desires good things, which in context has to be interpreted as the strong thesis that the desire for good is a standing motive, which requires to be focused in one direction or another via a conception of the overall good. Given that focus, desire is locked onto the target which is picked out by the conception, without the possibility of interference by conflicting desires. Hence all that is required for correct conduct is the correct focus, which has to be a correct conception of the agent's overall good.

On this theory motivation is uniform, and uniformly self-interested; every agent always aims at what he or she takes to be best for him- or herself, and failure to achieve that aim has to be explained by failure to grasp it properly, that is, by a cognitive defect, not by any defect of motivation. Socrates spells this out in *Protagoras*, on the assumption, which he attributes to people generally, that the agent's overall interest is to be defined in hedonistic terms, as the life which gives the best available balance of pleasure over distress. Given that assumption, it is nonsense to explain doing wrong by being overcome by pleasure or by any kind of desire; one must simply have made a mistake in one's estimation of what would bring the most pleasure. As Socrates says (358d), 'It is not in human nature to be prepared to go for what you think to be bad in preference to what is good.' There is considerable disagreement among commentators as to whether Socrates is represented as accepting the hedonistic assumption himself or merely as assuming it *ad hominem* to show that Protagoras has no view other than common opinion, but there is no doubt that, independently of that question, the view that the agent's conception of the good is the unique focus of motivation (maintained also in *Meno*) is Socrates' own. This account of goodness as knowledge thus issues directly in one of the claims for which Socrates was notorious in antiquity, the denial of the possibility of action against the agent's better judgement (*akrasia*); in Aristotle's words (*Nicomachean Ethics* 1145^{b}26–7) Socrates used to maintain that 'no one acts contrary to what is best in the belief that he is doing so, but through error', a thesis expressed more concisely in the slogan 'No one goes wrong intentionally' (*oudeis hekōn hamartanei* (*Prot.* 345e)).

Thus far the theory identifies goodness with the property which guarantees overall success in life, and identifies that property, via the motivational theory just described, with knowledge of what is best for the agent. But that theory lacks moral content; nothing in it shows or even suggests that what is best for the agent is to live a morally good life, as defined by the practice of the traditional virtues, including justice, with its implications of regard for others, and self-control, with its implications of the sacrifice of self-gratification. But if anything is characteristic of Socrates it is his insistence on the pre-eminence of morality. We saw that in the *Apology* he says that he knows that, come what may, he must not do wrong by disobeying the divine command to philosophize, and in *Crito* the fundamental thesis that one must never do wrong (or 'commit injustice' (*adikein*)) is the determining principle of his decision not to attempt escape from prison (49a–b). The link with the motivational thesis is established by the thesis that the best life for the agent is a life lived in accordance with the requirements of morality. Given that thesis, the slogan that no one goes wrong intentionally takes on the moral dimension that 'no one willingly does wrong (or 'acts unjustly'), but all who do wrong do so involuntarily' (or 'unintentionally') (*Gorg.* 509e), the full moral version of what has become known as the 'Socratic paradox'.

The thesis that the moral life is the best life *for the agent* thus has the central role of linking Socrates' intuitions of the pre-eminence of morality with the theory of uniform self-interested motivation which is the foundation of the identification of goodness with knowledge. It is the keystone of the entire arch. Given that centrality, it is surprising how little argumentative support it receives. At *Crito* 47e justice and injustice are described as respectively the health and sickness of the soul; hence, just as it is not worth living with a diseased and corrupted body, so it is not worth living with a diseased and corrupted soul. But that is not an argument. Even granted that health is an intrinsically desirable and disease an intrinsically undesirable state, the crucial claims that justice is the health of the soul, and injustice its disease, require defence, not mere assertion.

Plato supplies some arguments in *Gorgias*, but they are weak. Against Polus Socrates argues that successful tyrants, who, it is agreed, manifest the extremes of injustice, do not secure the best life for themselves, as Polus claims. On the contrary, they never get what they really want, because what they want is to do well for themselves, whereas their injustice is bad for them. The proof that it is bad for them (473e–475c) starts from Polus' admission that acting unjustly, while good (*agathon*) for the agent, is disgraceful (*aischron*). Socrates then secures agreement to the principle that whatever is disgraceful is so either because it is unpleasant, or because it is disadvantageous. Acting unjustly is clearly not unpleasant; hence by the above premises it must be disadvantageous. Hence a life of injustice is bad for the agent. Of the many weaknesses of this argument the crucial one is its neglect of the relativity of the concepts. To be acceptable the first premiss must be read as 'Whatever is disgraceful to anyone, is so either because it is unpleasant to someone or because it is disadvantageous to someone.' Given that premiss, it obviously does not follow that, because injustice is not unpleasant to the unjust person it must be disadvantageous to that person; it could be disadvantageous to someone else, and its being so could be the ground of its being disgraceful to the unjust person. (Indeed, one of the main reasons why we think that injustice is disgraceful to the perpetrator is that it is typically harmful to someone else.) Later in the dialogue (503e–504d) Socrates argues against Callicles that, since the goodness of anything (e.g. a boat or a house) depends on the proper proportion and order of its components, the goodness of both body and soul must depend on the proper proportion and order of their components, respectively health for the body and justice and self-control for the soul. The parallelism of bodily health and virtue, which was simply asserted in

Crito, is here supported by the general principle that goodness depends on organization of components, but that principle is insufficient to establish the parallelism. For the proper organization of components is itself determined by the function of the kind of thing in question; it is by considering that the function of a boat is to convey its occupants safely and conveniently by water that we determine whether its parts are put together well or badly. So in order to know which arrangement of psychological components such as intellect and bodily desires is optimum we need first to know what our aims in life ought to be. One conception of those aims may indeed identify the optimum organization as that defined by the conventional virtues, but another, for example, that of Don Juan or Gauguin, may identify a quite different organization, such as one which affords the maximum play to certain kinds of self-expression, as optimum.

The doctrine that virtue is knowledge is the key to understanding the so-called thesis of the Unity of the Virtues, maintained by Socrates in *Protagoras*. In that dialogue Protagoras assumes a broadly traditional picture of the virtues as a set of attributes distinct from one another, as, for example, the different bodily senses are distinct. A properly functioning human being has to have them all in proper working order, but it is possible to have some while lacking others; most notably, it is possible to possess conspicuous courage while being grossly deficient in respect of the other virtues (329d–e). Socrates suggests that, on the contrary, the names of the individual virtues, courage, self-control, etc., are all 'names of one and the same thing' (329c–d), and later in the dialogue makes it clear how that is to be understood by claiming (361b) that he has been 'trying to show that all things, justice, self-control, and courage, are knowledge'. The sense in which each of the virtues is knowledge is that, given the motivational theory sketched above, knowledge of what is best for the agent is necessary and sufficient to guarantee right conduct in whatever aspect of life that knowledge is applied to. We should not think of the individual virtues as different species of a generic knowledge; on that model piety is

66

knowledge of religious matters and courage is knowledge to do with what is dangerous, and the two are as different as, for example, knowledge of arithmetic and knowledge of geometry, which are distinct species of mathematical knowledge, allowing the possibility that one might have one without the other. The Socratic picture is that there is a single integrated knowledge, knowledge of what is best for the agent, which is applied in various areas of life, and to which the different names are applied with reference to those different areas. Thus, courage is the virtue which reliably produces appropriate conduct in situations of danger, piety the virtue which reliably produces appropriate conduct in relation to the gods, etc., and the virtue in question is the same in every case, namely, the agent's grasp of his or her good.

It has been objected[7] that this integrated picture is inconsistent with Socrates' acceptance in *Laches* and *Meno* that the individual virtues are parts of total virtue. In *Laches*, indeed, the proposed definition of courage as knowledge of what is fearful and not (194e–195a) is rejected on the ground that on that account courage would just be the knowledge of what is good and bad. But then courage would be identical with virtue as a whole, whereas *ex hypothesi* courage is not the whole, but a part of virtue (198a–199e). Given the aporetic nature of the dialogue, it is unclear whether at the time of writing Plato himself believed that the definition of courage was incompatible with the thesis that courage is a part of virtue, and, if so, whether he had a clear view on which should be abandoned. It is perfectly conceivable that he himself believed that they were not incompatible, and that the reader is being challenged to see that the rejection of the definition is not in fact required. What is clear is that the talk of parts of virtue can be given a straightforward interpretation which is compatible with the integrated picture. This is simply that total virtue extends over the whole of life, while 'courage', 'piety', etc. designate that virtue, not in respect of its total application, but in respect of its application to a restricted area. Similarly, coastal navigation and oceanic navigation are not two sciences, but a single science applied to different situations. Yet they can count as parts of navigation, in that competence in navigation requires mastery of both.[8]

The theory that virtue is knowledge is, as we have seen, flawed, in that one of its central propositions, that virtue is always in the agent's interest, is nowhere adequately supported in the Socratic dialogues. It also has a deeper flaw in that it is incoherent. The incoherence emerges when we ask 'What is virtue knowledge of?' The answer indicated by *Meno* and *Protagoras* is that virtue is knowledge of the agent's good, in that, given the standing motivation to achieve one's good, knowledge of what that good is will be necessary if one is to pursue it reliably, and sufficient to guarantee that the pursuit is successful. But that requires that the agent's good is something distinct from the knowledge which guarantees that one will achieve that good. 'Virtue is knowledge of the agent's good' is parallel to 'Medicine is knowledge of health'. Given that parallel, the value of virtue, the knowledge which guarantees the achievement of the good, will be purely instrumental, as the value of medicine is, and derivative from the intrinsic value of what it guarantees, that is, success in life (*eudaimonia*). But Socrates, as we saw, regards virtue as intrinsically, not merely instrumentally, valuable, and explicitly treats it as parallel, not to medicine, but to health itself. Virtue is, then, not a means to some independently specifiable condition of life which we can identify as *eudaimonia*; rather, it is a constituent of it (indeed, one of the trickiest questions about Socratic ethics is whether Socrates recognizes any other constituents). So, far from its being the case that virtue is worth pursuing because it is a means to a fully worthwhile life (e.g. a life of happiness), the order of explanation is reversed, in that a life is a life worth living either solely or at least primarily in virtue of the fact that it is a life of virtue.

The incoherence of the theory thus consists in the fact that Socrates maintains both that virtue is knowledge of what the agent's good is and that it is that good itself, whereas those two theses are inconsistent with one another. It could, of course, be the case both that virtue is knowledge of what the agent's good is, and that the agent's good is knowledge, but in that case the knowledge which is the agent's good has to be a distinct item or body of knowledge from the knowledge of what the agent's good is. Otherwise we have the situation that the knowledge of what the agent's good is is the knowledge that the agent's good is the knowledge of what the agent's good is, and that that knowledge (i.e. the knowledge of what the agent's good is) is in turn the knowledge that the agent's good is the knowledge of what the agent's good is, and so on *ad infinitum*. *So*, if Socrates wishes to stick to the claim that virtue is knowledge he must either specify that knowledge as knowledge of something other than what the agent's good is, or he must give up the thesis that virtue is the agent's good.

Plato represents Socrates as grappling with this problem in *Euthydemus*. This dialogue presents a confrontation between two conceptions of philosophy, represented respectively by Socrates and by a pair of sophists, the brothers Euthydemus and Dionysodorus. The latter demonstrate their conception by putting on a dazzling display of the techniques of fallacious argument which enable them to 'combat in argument and refute whatever anyone says, whether it is true or false' (272a–b). For his part Socrates seeks to argue for the central role of wisdom in the achievement of *eudaimonia*. The first part of his argument (278e–281e) is in essence the same as that used in *Meno* 87d–89a to establish that virtue is knowledge; knowledge or wisdom (the terms are interchangeable) is the only unconditionally good thing, since all other goods, whether goods of fortune or desirable traits of character, are good for the agent only if they are properly used, and they are properly used only if they are directed by wisdom. Thus far Socrates reproduces the position of *Meno*, but in the second part of his argument (288d–292e) he goes beyond it. Here he points out that the previous argument has shown that the skill which secures the overall good of the agent is one which co-ordinates the production and use of all subordinate goods, including the products of all other skills. It is thus a directive or governing skill, which is appropriately termed the political or kingly (*basilikē*) art. But now what is the goal of the kingly art? Not to provide goods such as wealth or freedom for people, for the previous argument has shown that those are good only on the condition that they are directed by wisdom. So the goal of the kingly art can only be to make people wise. But wise at what? Not wise (= skilled) at shoemaking or building, for the same reason, that those skills are good only if they are directed by the supreme skill. The goal of the kingly art can therefore be none other than to make people skilled in the kingly art itself. But, as Socrates admits (292d–e), that is completely uninformative, since we lack any conception of what the kingly art is.

Socrates leaves the puzzle unresolved, and it may well be that at that point Plato did not see his way out of the puzzle. What this dialogue does show is that Plato had become aware of the incoherence of the system of Socratic ethics whose two central tenets are that virtue is knowledge (sc. of human good) and that virtue is human good. If human good is to be identified with both knowledge and virtue, then that knowledge must have some object other than itself. Plato's eventual solution was to develop (in the *Republic*) a conception of human good as consisting in a state of the personality in which the non-rational impulses are directed by the intellect informed by knowledge, not of human good, but of goodness itself, a universal principle of rationality. On this conception (i) human good is virtue, (ii) virtue is, not identical with, but directed by, knowledge, and (iii) the knowledge in question is knowledge of the universal good. It is highly plausible to see *Euthydemus* as indicating the transition from the Socratic position set out most explicitly in *Meno* to that developed Platonic position.

Protagoras may be seen as an exploration of another solution to this puzzle, since in that dialogue Socrates sets out an account of goodness whose central theses are: (i) virtue is knowledge of human good (as in *Meno*); (ii) human good is an overall pleasant life. The significance of this is independent of whether Socrates is represented as adopting that solution in his own person, or merely as proposing it as a theory which ordinary people and Protagoras ought to accept. Either way, it represents a way out of the impasse which blocks the original form of the Socratic theory, though not a way which Plato was himself to adopt. Having experimented with this theory, which retains the identity of virtue with knowledge while abandoning the identity of virtue with human good, he settled for the alternative just described, which maintains the latter identity while abandoning the former.

Socrates and the Sophists

The confrontation of Socrates with sophists is central to Plato's apologetic project. Socrates, as we have seen, had been tarred with the sophistic brush, and it was therefore central to the defence of his memory to show how wide the gap was between his activity and that of the sophists. Since Socrates represents in Plato's presentation the ideal philosopher, the confrontation can also be seen more abstractly, as a clash between genuine philosophy and its counterfeit.

Plato depicts Socrates in confrontation with sophists and their associates in the three longest and dramatically most complex dialogues of the group which we are considering: *Gorgias*, *Protagoras*, and *Euthydemus*. I shall consider those together with *Republic* 1, which may originally have been a separate dialogue; even if it was not, it certainly looks back to the aporetic and elenctic style of the earlier dialogues, while there are obvious similarities between the positions of Callicles in *Gorgias* and Thrasymachus in *Republic* 1. As well as these major dramatic dialogues, Socrates is presented in one-to-one discussion with a sophist in the two *Hippias* dialogues.

The Greek word *sophistēs* (formed from the adjective *sophos* 'wise' or 'learned') originally meant 'expert' or 'sage'; thus the famous Seven Sages were referred to as the 'Seven *Sophistai*'. In the fifth century it came to be applied particularly to the new class of itinerant intellectuals, such as Protagoras and Hippias, whom we find depicted in the Socratic dialogues. We saw earlier that sophists were regarded in some quarters as dangerous subversives, overthrowing conventional religion and morality by a combination of naturalistic science and argumentative trickery. Plato presents a much more nuanced picture. There are indeed elements of subversion, in that both Callicles and Thrasymachus mount powerful attacks on conventional morality. As for argumentative trickery, Euthydemus and Dionysodorus are shameless in their deliberate bamboozling of opponents. But Plato is far from presenting sophists as a class as either moral subversives or argumentative charlatans, much less as both. In *Protagoras* the sophist represents his own teaching of the art of life not as critical of conventional social morality but as continuous with it, since he takes over where traditional education leaves off. He defends traditional morality, and in particular the central role which it assigns to the basic social virtues of justice and self-control, by a story designed to show how it is a natural development, determined by the necessity of social co-operation if humans are to survive in a hostile world. He argues sensibly and in some places effectively for his views. Interestingly, neither his claim to make the weaker argument the stronger nor his agnosticism on the existence and nature of the gods gets any mention in this portrayal. Prodicus, who also appears in *Protagoras* and is mentioned fairly often in other Platonic dialogues, is said to have given naturalistic accounts of the origin of religion and was accounted an atheist by some ancient writers, but this is nowhere mentioned by Plato, whose primary interest is in making fun of his penchant for nice verbal distinctions. Hippias is presented both in *Protagoras* and in the *Hippias* dialogues as a polymath, whose interests range from science and astronomy to history, literary criticism, and mnemonics. In *Hippias Major* he has little capacity for following an argument, and there is no suggestion in any of these dialogues of radical views on anything. Gorgias starts out by claiming that rhetoric, his field of expertise, is a value-free discipline (455a), but is trapped by Socrates into acknowledging that a good orator must know what is just and unjust, and that if his pupils do not know this already they will learn it from him (460a). There is no indication of what his substantive views on justice and injustice may have been; specifically, there is no suggestion in the dialogue that Callicles has derived his immoralism from Gorgias. It would give a better fit with what is plainly meant to be Gorgias' real position if any influence that Gorgias may have had on Callicles were restricted to the rhetorical force which he manifests in such abundance in expressing his atrocious views. In Plato's eyes that influence was no less dangerous than positive indoctrination.

It is worth pointing out that Plato's presentation of the personalities of the sophists is as nuanced as his treatment of their doctrines. At least, they are not portrayed in a tone of uniform hostility. Thrasymachus, indeed, is a thoroughly nasty piece of work: arrogant, rude, and aggressive (he even tells Socrates to get his nurse to wipe his nose and stop his drivelling (343a)), and Hippias is a learned and conceited blockhead, but the others are treated more gently. The charlatanry of the brothers in *Euthydemus* is so transparent as to be almost endearing, while Prodicus is a figure of rather gentle fun. Protagoras, on the other hand, is a much more considerable figure; he is certainly pompous and complacent, and he does get ruffled when he loses the argument, but he quickly recovers his poise and concludes with a generous, if slightly patronizing, compliment to Socrates. More significantly, Plato presents him as someone to be taken seriously intellectually. The speech which sets out his defence of social morality and his role as an educator is a serious piece of work, and up to the concluding argument he is represented as holding his own in debate with Socrates. When we add to this the lengthy critique of his doctrines in *Theaetetus* (something which has no parallel in the case of any other sophist) it is clear that Plato took him very seriously indeed.

Plato's Socrates is not interested in the religious unorthodoxy of the sophists. (Later, in book 10 of the *Laws*, Plato argues strongly that atheism leads to immorality, and recommends institutional means of suppressing it – including the death penalty for those who persist in it – but that is a stance foreign to the Platonic Socrates.) He faces a serious challenge from one strand of sophistic moral thinking, represented by Thrasymachus, who is himself a sophist, and Callicles, who is an associate of Gorgias. The basis of those views, explicit in Callicles, implicit in Thrasymachus, is the dichotomy between what is natural and what is merely conventional. Both assume an egoistic view of human nature, maintaining that, in common with other animals, humans have a natural tendency to seek the maximum self-gratification, from which they conclude that, for the individual, success in life (*eudaimonia*) consists in giving that tendency free play. Law and morality they see as conventional devices for restricting that natural tendency with a view to promoting the good of others; their effect is to force people to sacrifice their own *eudaimonia* in favour of that of others. But since everyone has more reason to favour their own *eudaimonia* over that of others, the rational course for everyone is to free themselves from the shackles of law and morality. (Callicles goes a step further in claiming that that is not merely rational but in reality right or just (*phusei dikaion*), since the individual who is strong enough to exploit others is thereby entitled to do so, and is wronged by laws or conventions which seek to prevent him.)

The moral theory sketched in the previous chapter provided a response to this challenge, though a weak one, since the crucial link between morality and the agent's good was not established. But in addition to this radical challenge to conventional morality, the sophistic tradition provided an argument in support of it, and thereby an answer to the challenge, in the form of the theory of the social origin of morality expounded by Protagoras in the dialogue (see above). This theory rejects the fundamental thesis of the radicals that nature and convention are opposed. On the contrary, convention, in the form of social morality, is itself a product of nature, since it naturally comes about when human beings are obliged to adapt (by forming communities) in order to survive. So far from its being the case that convention stultifies the development of human nature, it is only via convention that human nature is able to survive and flourish, in the sense of developing civilization.

To the extent that Protagoras upholds conventional morality, especially justice and self-control, he is an ally against Callicles and Thrasymachus. For all that, Socrates finds his theory inadequate. He could have made the point, though he does not in fact, that Protagoras' account makes justice and self-control only instrumentally instead of intrinsically desirable; their value lies in their necessity as prerequisites for the benefits of communal life, but what is necessary is that those virtues should be generally, rather than universally, cultivated. Hence someone who can get away with wrongdoing on a particular occasion without endangering the social fabric has no reason not to do so (the 'free-rider' problem). That issue is addressed in book 2 of the *Republic*. In *Protagoras* Socrates' criticism is that, in assuming the separateness of the individual virtues (see above), Protagoras manifests an inadequate grasp of the nature of goodness. Hence his claim to expertise about goodness (in other words, to teach *politikē technē* (319a)) is fraudulent, and those, like Hippocrates, who flock to him in the expectation of acquiring goodness, are not merely wasting their time and money, but are risking the positive harm of acquiring a mistaken view of goodness and hence a mistaken conception of their proper goal in life (312b–314b).

Sophists, then, are dangerous, but not in the way that they are conceived in the popular caricature. They are a threat, not primarily because they peddle atheism or immorality (though some sophists did promote one or the other), but because they set themselves up as experts on the most important question, 'How is one to live?' without actually having the requisite knowledge. This is the recurrent theme of

Socrates' confrontations with them. Protagoras claims to teach people how to acquire goodness, but proves to have no grasp of what it is. Euthydemus and Dionysodorus make precisely the same claim (275a), but all they actually have to teach is verbal trickery. (Protagoras is clearly represented as making his claim in good faith, but the same can hardly be said for the brothers. The point is immaterial; whether or not the sophist believes his claim, the important point is that it is unfounded.) Hippias claims universal expertise, including expertise on the nature of the fine or beautiful, an aspect of goodness, but his claim proves as hollow as those of the others. Socrates, by contrast, does not normally claim to have expertise. What he represents is the true conception of the task of philosophy, which is to search for genuine expertise in the art of life. What that expertise is is the possession of the true account of goodness, and hence the true account of our proper aim in life.

This conception of philosophy is emphasized in *Gorgias* via the contrast with rhetoric. The art of life (*politikē*) seeks the good, which requires knowledge of what the good is, whereas rhetoric aims merely at gratifying the desires of people who lack knowledge of whether the satisfaction of those desires is good or not. Hence the true expert in the art of life is the philosopher, represented by Socrates, who here, exceptionally, does claim expertise. If, instead of being guided by philosophy, people's lives are ruled by rhetoric, the result is the substitution of the pursuit of pleasure for that of the good, a situation which can lead to the moral chaos represented by Callicles, for whom the good is the indiscriminate pursuit of every pleasure. Gorgias, it seems, does not himself claim to teach goodness, unlike the sophists; the dialogue is then, unlike the others we have discussed, a critique not of an unfounded claim to expertise, but of the misguided practice (characteristic, in Plato's view, of Athenian democracy) of assigning to the technique of persuasion the role which properly belongs to philosophical enquiry, that of identifying fundamental values.

Chapter 5
Socrates and Later Philosophy

Ancient Philosophy

From the modern perspective by far the most important legacy of Socrates was his influence on Plato. But we have seen that Plato was one of a number of associates who wrote about him in the generation immediately after his death and who were themselves influenced by him in one way or another. In this section I shall trace briefly the main ways in which the influence of Socrates was transmitted to later generations, by personal association and via the writings of Plato and others.

We may begin with two personal associates of Socrates, Antisthenes and Aristippus. Antisthenes is said to have been originally a pupil of Gorgias who transferred his allegiance to Socrates. He appears to have been a sophist in the traditional style, who wrote on a wide range of subjects, many of them remote from the interests of Socrates, who concentrated on ethics. His interests in the nature of language and its relation to reality, and in particular his denial of the possibility of contradiction, link him rather with Socrates' sophistic opponents, notably Prodicus and Protagoras, both of whom are said to have maintained that thesis. He thus appears as an eclectic figure, in whom the specifically Socratic influence is manifested in his adherence to some of Socrates' ethical doctrines and in his austere style of life. He maintained that goodness can be taught and that it is sufficient for happiness, adding the significant rider 'requiring nothing more in addition than Socratic strength' (DL 6.10–11). The rider suggests a shift from the Socratic denial of the possibility of *akrasia* (action against one's better judgement); knowledge of the agent's good does not by itself guarantee pursuit of it, as Socrates had held, but in addition the agent must acquire sufficient strength to adhere to his or her judgement of what is best, which implies that that judgement needs to be defended against the possibility of erosion by conflicting desires. (Plato indicates a similar modification at *Rep*. 429c, where he defines courage as 'retention, amid pleasures and desires and fears, of the belief inculcated by law and education about what is fearful and what is not'.) Socratic strength was to be promoted by a life of physical austerity, eschewing all pleasures except those appropriate to such a life. It thus appears that that aspect of Socrates' life-style was as significant an influence on Antisthenes as his doctrines. Subsequently, extreme austerity became the trademark of the Cynics, who combined it with rejection of normal social conventions as an expression of their central tenet that the good was life in conformity with nature. Later Antisthenes was said to have been the founder of the Cynic sect. Rather than any doctrinal or organizational influence, of which there is no evidence, this reflects the tradition of the transmission of the Socratic life-style, as Diogenes Laertius explicitly reports (6.2): Antisthenes, he says, 'taking over his endurance from him [i.e. Socrates] and emulating his immunity from feeling became the founder of Cynicism'.

Aristippus was a native of Cyrene in North Africa who was attracted to Athens by the reputation of Socrates. He, too, wrote in a number of areas, including ethics, theory of language, and history, and is said to have been the first of Socrates' associates to follow the sophists' practice of charging fees for teaching. He is reputed to have been the founder of the Cyrenaic school, which was influential in the fourth and third centuries BC, but since all our information about Cyrenaic doctrine dates from after the foundation of the school there is no reliable

8. A detail from Raphael's *The School of Athens* (1508–11), which portrays the most famous thinkers of ancient Greece. Plato and Aristotle are in the centre, with Socrates to the left of them, addressing a group of bystanders.

indication whether any of its doctrines were maintained by Aristippus himself. The principal tenets of the school were the ethical doctrine that the sensory pleasure of the present moment is the supreme good, and the epistemological doctrine that the only things that can be known are present sense-impressions. These are connected by the sceptical implications of the latter. By that doctrine the past and the future are equally inaccessible; hence the only rational aim is some feature of present experience. The claim of pleasure to be that feature was supported by the argument that all living things pursue pleasure and shun pain. Uniquely among Greek philosophers the Cyrenaics rejected the claim of *eudaimonia* to be the supreme good, on the strength of this sceptical argument; *eudaimonia* involves assessing life as a whole, but such assessment is impossible given the unknowability of anything but the present. Hence the wise person's goal should be, not *eudaimonia*, but the pleasure of the moment.

It is hard to see much trace of Socratic influence in these doctrines. The doctrine that the supreme good is the pleasure of the moment is closer to the view of Callicles than to that of Socrates, and though some later sceptics claimed Socrates as their ancestor, that was not on the strength of the thesis that the only knowable things are current sense-impressions, which is a version of the Protagorean position criticized in *Theaetetus*. On the other hand, some evidence of the views of Aristippus preserved by Eusebius suggests something closer to recognizably Socratic positions. According to this, he taught that pleasure is to be pursued, not unconditionally, but provided it does not endanger self-control, which results from education, self-knowledge, study, and endurance (*karteria*), the very word which was the key term in Antisthenes' ascetic morality. It is then plausible to suggest that the doctrine that momentary pleasure is the supreme good represents a position developed by the school, subsequent to the time of Aristippus himself, when the influence of sceptical doctrines had become more prominent.

Most of the ancient biographical evidence about Aristippus concerns his luxurious mode of life, and he appears in that aspect in Xenophon's *Memorabilia*, where Socrates admonishes him by telling him Prodicus' fable of the Choice of Heracles (2.1). The moral of this is the broadly Antisthenean one that a life of simplicity and hard toil brings greater pleasure in the long run than a life of luxury. The appeal is to long-term considerations, and there is no suggestion that Aristippus has any theoretical grounds for rejecting that appeal. We might then suggest that the contrast between Antisthenes and Aristippus may not have been an extreme doctrinal antithesis, but rather a matter of temperament, Antisthenes being attracted by the ascetic aspects of Socrates' life to the extent of elevating them to the status of a moral ideal, while Aristippus may have felt that the Socratic ideals of self-knowledge and self-control could be accommodated to a more easy-going way of life. It is worth recalling some less stern aspects of the figure of Socrates, such as his exceptional capacity to enjoy food and drink (Pl. *Symp.* 220a), and his erotic reputation. The hedonistic Socrates presented in *Protagoras* may have been taken by some to represent his actual views, as is suggested by the papyrus mentioned above, where Socrates is counted among those who think that pleasure is the best goal in life. It is a striking fact (commented on by Augustine (*City of God* 8.3)) that the figure of Socrates was sufficiently plastic to allow two such contrasting life-styles as those of Antisthenes and Aristippus both to count as in certain respects Socratic.

The connection of Socrates with the Cynics via Antisthenes developed into a connection with Stoicism, since the Stoics saw themselves as heirs both of the Cynics and of Socrates. The succession of leaders of the schools drawn up by Hellenistic historians (exhibited in the order of lives in DL 6–7) runs from Antisthenes via Diogenes of Sinope (who was described as 'Socrates gone mad' (DL 6.54)) and Crates to Zeno of Citium, the founder of Stoicism; Zeno is said to have been converted to philosophy by reading Xenophon's *Memorabilia* on a visit to Athens, and to have asked where he could find someone like Socrates, in answer to which he was advised to associate with Crates. From the Cynics the Stoics took the central doctrine of the life according to nature as the supreme human good. It was, however, Socrates rather than the Cynics whom they took to reveal what the life according to nature consisted in. For the Stoics, the life according to nature was the life appropriate to each kind of living thing, whereby it fitted into its place in the perfect order of nature as a whole. Human beings are rational creatures, and life according to nature for humans is therefore life in accordance with reason. Since there is no distinction of rational and non-rational elements in the human soul, there is no distinction between moral virtue and rationality. The Stoics thus accepted the cardinal doctrines of Socratic ethics, that virtue is knowledge, and that virtue is sufficient for *eudaimonia*. The doctrine of *Meno* and *Euthydemus* that virtue (= knowledge) is the only unconditional good they interpreted in the strong sense that virtue is the only good, everything else being 'indifferent', that is, neither good nor bad. Aristo, a follower of Zeno, maintained the thesis of the Unity of the Virtues, interpreting it as the thesis that the names of the different virtues are alternative characterizations of the knowledge of good and bad, differentiated by reference to the relation of that knowledge to different circumstances.

The Stoics thus held both the doctrines which we saw to lead to an impasse in Socratic ethics, that virtue is knowledge (sc. of the good) and that virtue is the only good, and their critics were not slow to claim that they too had no escape: Plutarch alleges (*Common Notions* 1072b) that when asked what the good is they say 'Nothing but intelligence' and when asked what intelligence is say 'Nothing but knowledge of goods', referring directly to the passage in *Euthydemus* (292e) where the difficulty was originally raised. But their doctrine that human goodness is conformity with the perfect order of nature gives them an escape route. Human goodness is knowledge of goodness indeed, but it is not thereby knowledge of nothing other than human goodness, that is, knowledge of itself. It is knowledge of the goodness of the universe, i.e. conformity to the goodness of the universe by the realization of perfect rationality in the soul. But now it seems that the difficulty has been merely postponed; for rationality has to consist in making the right choices, that is, choices of what is good in preference to what is bad, and if nothing is good or bad but virtue and vice respectively we have after all no informative account of what goodness is. This problem exercised the Stoics, some of whom sought to find a solution in a distinction among 'indifferent' things between 'preferred indifferents' such as health and 'unpreferred indifferents' such as sickness. Neither kind of indifferent is better or worse than the other, but nature prompts us to seek the preferred and shun the unpreferred, and goodness consists in making the right choices in accordance with these natural promptings. Critics such as Plutarch (*Stoic Contradictions* 1047-8) claimed that by this manoeuvre the Stoics were attempting to have their cake and eat it, in that they had to claim that the choice of indifferents was both a matter of the utmost concern and a matter of no concern at all. The many fascinating issues which this raises cannot be pursued here.

The dependence in Stoic thought of human goodness on the rational order of the universe presented a special difficulty for their claim to follow Socrates, in that it makes knowledge of nature prior to ethical knowledge, whereas Socrates had famously eschewed interest in natural philosophy and confined himself to ethics (Xen. *Mem.* 1. 1. 16, Aristotle *Metaphysics* 987^{b}1-2). Yet they could find passages in Xenophon's *Memorabilia* where Socrates draws moral implications from general considerations about nature. In 1.4 Socrates seeks to convert the atheist Aristodemus by arguing for the existence of the gods and their care for humans from the providential design of the human body. In the course of this discussion he argues that human intelligence must be a portion of a larger quantity of intelligence pervading the world, just as the physical elements which compose the human body are portions of the larger totalities of those elements; later he says that the intelligence which is in the universe organizes everything as best pleases it and that the divine sees and hears everything and is everywhere and takes care of everything all at once. This certainly can be read as foreshadowing the Stoic picture of the cosmos as itself a divine, intelligent, self-organizing being, and both Cicero (*De Natura Deorum* 2.6.18) and Sextus (*Adversus Mathematicos* 9.92–104) refer explicitly to this passage of Xenophon as a source of Stoic argument for cosmic rationality. (A similar argument occurs in *Memorabilia* 4.3, with special reference to the gods' care for humans as evinced in their conferring rationality and language on them.) Another passage of *Memorabilia* which strikingly anticipates Stoic doctrine is 4.4, where Socrates and Hippias agree that there are some universal, unwritten moral laws, for example, that one should worship the gods and honour one's parents, which are not the product of human convention as are the laws of particular communities, but are laid down by the gods for all men, and sanctioned by inevitable punishment. For a detailed Stoic parallel (so close as to raise the possibility of imitation) see Cicero, *Republic* 3.33.

According to the first-century BC Epicurean Philodemus the Stoics wished to be called Socratics, and Socrates remained a paradigm of the sage throughout their history. His acceptance of death was a model of how the wise man should confront death, as is reflected in descriptions of famous Stoic suicides such as that of Seneca. To Epictetus, writing in the first and second centuries AD, he is the sage *par excellence*, whose influence he sums up in the words 'Now that Socrates is dead, the memory of what he did or said when alive is no less or even more beneficial to men' (*Discourses* 4.1.169).

There were two principal traditions of philosophical scepticism in antiquity, the Pyrrhonians and the Academics. The former traced their philosophical ancestry from the fourth-century Pyrrho of Elis, who like Socrates wrote nothing himself and for that reason remains a somewhat elusive figure. There is no firm evidence that adherents of this school regarded Socrates as a sceptic. In the works of Sextus

Empiricus, who is our principal source for Pyrrhonian scepticism, Socrates is almost invariably listed among the dogmatists, that is, those who maintained positive doctrines as opposed to suspending judgement on all questions as the sceptics recommended; only once (*Adversus Mathematicos* 7.264) is Socrates cited as suspending judgement, on the strength of his ironical statement at *Phaedrus* 230a that he is so far from self-knowledge that he does not know whether he is a man or a many-headed monster. For the Academics the situation was different. The Academy was Plato's own school, which embraced scepticism under the leadership of Arcesilaus just over a century after its foundation and remained a sceptical school for over two hundred years until it reverted to dogmatism under Antiochus of Ascalon. Arcesilaus claimed that in embracing scepticism he was remaining faithful to the spirit of both Socrates and Plato, whose philosophical practice he claimed to have been sceptical, not dogmatic.

Cicero, our main source, makes it clear that Arcesilaus saw Socrates' argumentative practice as purely negative and *ad hominem*; he maintained no doctrines himself, but merely asked others what they thought and argued against them. In the dialogues we do indeed find many cases where Socrates' interlocutors are brought to an impasse by the revelation of inconsistency in their beliefs; Arcesilaus interpreted this outcome as supporting the general sceptical position that there is nothing which the senses or the mind can grasp as certain (*De Oratore* 3.67; cf. *De Finibus* 2.2, 5.10). He attributed to Socrates the paradoxical claim that he knew nothing except this, that he knew nothing (*Academica* 1.45; cf. 2.74), and criticized him on the ground that he should not have claimed to know even that.

Our previous discussion should have made it clear that while Arcesilaus' reading of Socrates does pick out genuine features of his argumentative practice, it is unduly selective. His profession of ignorance is a denial that he possesses wisdom or expertise, which is compatible with the claims (a) that he knows some things in a non-expert way, and (b) that others know some things as experts. He neither claims that he knows nothing, nor does he claim that he knows that he knows nothing. He never draws from the negative outcome of his examinations of others the universal thesis that there is nothing which the senses or the mind can grasp as certain. On the contrary, he thinks that knowledge is identical with the good, and takes the negative outcome of his enquiries as a stimulus to the further search for it. Of course, the sceptic is entitled to maintain that the search for knowledge is not incompatible with scepticism. A *skeptikos* is a searcher, and the sceptic continually searches for knowledge, which constantly eludes him. But despite the claim to be engaged on an ongoing search for knowledge, the sceptic is committed to a general pessimism about the human capacity to achieve it; in Arcesilaus' version 'there is nothing which *can* [my emphasis] be grasped as certain by the mind or the senses'. It is not just that any enquiry so far undertaken has failed to reach certainty. The sceptic believes in advance that that will be the outcome on any occasion and has some general strategies, such as the appeal to conflicting appearances or arguments, to show that it must. There is no trace of that pessimism in Plato's portrayal of Socrates.

Not all subsequent philosophers were well disposed towards Socrates. Some of Aristotle's successors were hostile, notably Aristoxenus, whose malicious biography was the source of the story of Socrates' bigamy; it attracted a rejoinder from the Stoic Panaetius. The most consistent hostility came from the Epicureans. True to their tradition of abusive comments on non-Epicurean philosophers, a succession of Epicureans made rude remarks about Socrates. Typical of these are some remarks of Colotes which Plutarch cites, describing the story of the oracle given to Chaerephon as 'a completely cheap and sophistical tale' (*Against Colotes* 1116e–f), and Socrates' arguments as so much boasting or quackery (*alazonas*) on the ground that they were discordant with what he actually did (1117d; presumably Colotes had in mind some instances of Socrates' ironical professions of admiration of his interlocutors). As both the Stoics and the sceptical Academics were regarded by the Epicureans as professional rivals, it is plausible that the Epicureans' hostility to Socrates stemmed in part from the position which he was accorded by those schools.

The tendency to appropriate Socrates as a precursor was not restricted to pagan philosophers. Writing in the second century AD the Christian apologist Justin cited the example of Socrates in rebuttal of the accusation of atheism levelled at the Christians. Like them, he claimed, Socrates was accused of atheism because he rejected the fables of the Olympian gods and urged the worship of one true God. Socrates had thus had some partial grasp of the coming revelation through Christ, since, though philosophers are responsible for their own errors and contradictions through their limited grasp of the truth 'whatever has been well said by them belongs to us Christians'.

Medieval and Modern Philosophy

The Christianization of Socrates so strikingly expressed by Justin was not the beginning of a continuous tradition. Though Augustine was influenced by Plato to the extent of speculating that he might have known the Old Testament scriptures, he does not follow Justin in claiming Socrates for Christianity. While some Christian writers praise Socrates as a good man unjustly put to death, most of those who mention him refer with disapproval to his 'idolatry', citing his divine sign (interpreted by some, including Tertullian, as communications from a demon), his sacrifice to Asclepius, and his oaths 'By the dog', etc. To the extent that the Platonic tradition retained its vitality in the early medieval period it concentrated on later Platonic works, especially *Timaeus*, in which the personality of Socrates plays an insignificant role, and from the twelfth century onwards the influence of Plato was largely eclipsed in the West by that of Aristotle. The major medieval philosophers show little or no interest in Socrates, and it is not until the revival of Platonism in the late fifteenth century that any significant interest in him re-emerges. As part of the neo-Platonist

9. Frontispiece drawn by Matthew Paris of St Albans (*d.* 1259) for a fortune-telling tract, *The Prognostics of Socrates the King*. The pop-eyed appearance of the figure named 'Plato' and the fact that 'Socrates' is writing to 'Plato's' dictation suggests that the names have been transposed. The image appears on a postcard, referred to in the title of Jacques Derrida's work *La Carte Postale*.

programme of interpreting Platonism as an allegorical expression of
Christian truth we find the Florentine Marsilio Ficino drawing detailed
parallels between the trials and deaths of Socrates and Jesus, and this
tradition was continued by Erasmus (one of whose dialogues contains
the expression 'Saint Socrates, pray for us') in a comparison between
Christ in the garden of Gethsemane and Socrates in his condemned
cell. (The tradition was continued in subsequent centuries, by (among
others) Diderot and Rousseau in the eighteenth and various writers in
the nineteenth, all of them adjusting the parallelism to fit their
particular religious preconceptions.) As in the ancient world, the figure
of Socrates lent itself to appropriation by competing ideologies. For
Montaigne in the sixteenth century Socrates was not a Christ-figure
but a paradigm of natural virtue and wisdom, and the supernatural
elements in the ancient portrayal, particularly the divine sign, were to
be explained in naturalistic terms; the sign was perhaps a faculty of
instinctive, unreasoned decision, facilitated by his settled habits of
wisdom and virtue. The growth of a rationalizing approach to religion
in the seventeenth and eighteenth centuries, which rejected revelation
and the fanaticism consequent on disputes about its interpretation,
allowed Socrates to be seen as a martyr for rational religion, who had
met his death at the hands of fanatics. In this vein Voltaire wrote a
play on the death of Socrates, and the Deist John Toland composed
a liturgy for worship in a 'Socratic Sodality', including a litany in
which, following the example of Erasmus, the name of Socrates was
invoked.

As in the ancient world, there were dissenting voices. Some writers
were critical of Socrates' morals, citing his homosexual tendencies and
his neglect of his wife and children. For some, including Voltaire, the
divine sign manifested a regrettable streak of superstition. The
eighteenth century saw the appearance of the first modern works
reviving the claim that the charges against Socrates were political and
defending his condemnation on the basis of his hostility to Athenian
democracy and his associations with Critias and Alcibiades. (That line

of interpretation continues up to the present, one example being I. F. Stone's widely read *The Trial of Socrates*.) And some writers of orthodox Christian views repudiated the parallels between Socrates and Jesus, alleging, in addition to the charges of superstition and immorality already mentioned, that Socrates had in effect committed suicide.

The pattern of appropriation to an alien culture has parallels in the treatment of Socrates in medieval Arabic literature. Apart from Plato and Aristotle, he is the philosopher most frequently referred to by Arabic writers, and the interest in him extended beyond philosophers to poets, theologians, mystics, and other scholars. This interest was not founded on extensive knowledge of the relevant Greek texts. While works dealing with Socrates' death, notably Plato's *Phaedo* and *Crito*, were clearly well known, there is little evidence of wider knowledge of the Platonic dialogues, and none of knowledge of other Socratic literature. There was, however, an extensive tradition of anecdotes recording sayings of Socrates, of the kind recorded in Diogenes Laertius and other biographical and moralizing writers. This tradition represents Socrates as a sage, one of the 'Seven Pillars of Wisdom' (i.e. sages), a moral paragon, an exemplar of all the virtues, and a fount of wisdom on every topic, including man, the world, time, and, above all, God. He is consistently presented as maintaining an elaborate monotheistic theology, neo-Platonist in its details, and his condemnation and death are attributed to his upholding faith in the one true God against the errors of idolators. This allows him to be seen as a forerunner of Islamic sages (as he was seen in the West as a proto-Christian), and to be described in terms which assimilate him to figures venerated in Islam, including Abraham, Jesus, and even the Prophet himself. Some writings represent him as an ascetic, and it is clear that he is conflated with the Cynics, above all with Diogenes, even to the extent of living in a tub and telling Alexander the Great to step out of the light when he was sunbathing. In other writings he is the father of alchemy, in others again a pioneer in logic, mathematics, and physics.

Again, as in the West, the generally honorific perception of Socrates was challenged on religious grounds by some orthodox believers (such as the eleventh/twelfth-century theologian al-Ghazali), who represented him as a father of heresies, a threat to Islam, and even as an atheist.[9]

The tradition of adapting the figure of Socrates to fit the general preconceptions of the writer is discernible in his treatment by three major philosophers of the nineteenth century, Hegel, Kierkegaard, and Nietzsche. In his *Lectures on the History of Philosophy*, first delivered in 1805–6, Hegel sees the condemnation of Socrates as a tragic clash between two moral standpoints, each of which is justified, and thereby a necessary stage in the dialectical process by which the world-spirit realizes itself in its fullest development. Before Socrates the Athenians had spontaneously and unreflectively followed the dictates of objective morality (*Sittlichkeit*). By critically examining people's moral beliefs Socrates turns morality into something individual and reflective (*Moralität*); it is a requirement of this new morality that its principles stand the test of critical reflection on the part of the individual. Yet, since Socrates was unable to give any determinate account of the good, the effect of this critical reflection is merely to undermine the authority of *Sittlichkeit*. Critical reflection reveals that the exceptionless moral laws which *Sittlichkeit* had proclaimed have exceptions in fact, but the lack of a determinate criterion leaves the individual with no way of determining what is right in particular cases other than inward illumination or conscience, which in Socrates' case takes the form of his divine sign.

Socrates' appeal to his conscience is thus an appeal to an authority higher than that of the collective moral sense of the people, but that is an appeal which the people cannot allow:

> The spirit of this people in itself, its constitution, its whole life, rested, however, on a moral ground, on religion, and could not exist without

this absolutely secure basis. Thus because Socrates makes the truth rest on the judgement of inward consciousness, he enters upon a struggle with the Athenian people as to what is right and true. His accusation was therefore just.

(i. 426)[10]

The clash between individual conscience and the state was therefore inevitable, in that both necessarily claim supreme moral authority. It is also tragic, in that both sides are right:

In what is truly tragic there must be valid moral powers on both the sides which come into collision; this was so with Socrates. The one power is the divine right, the natural morality whose laws are identical with the will which dwells therein as in its own essence, freely and nobly; we may call it abstractly objective freedom. The other principle, on the contrary, is the right, as really divine, of consciousness or of subjective freedom: this is the fruit of the tree of knowledge of good and evil, i.e. of self-creative reason; and it is the universal principle for all successive times. It is these two principles which we see coming into opposition in the life and philosophy of Socrates.

(i. 446–7)

The situation is tragic in that both the collective morality of the people and the individual conscience make demands on the individual which are justified and ineluctable, but conflicting: the only resolution is the development of humanity to a stage in which these demands necessarily coincide. The individual nonconformist such as Socrates is defeated, but that defeat leads to the triumph of what that 'false individuality' imperfectly represented, the critical activity of the world-spirit:

The false form of individuality is taken away, and that, indeed, in a violent way, by punishment, but the principle itself will penetrate later, if in another form, and elevate itself into a form of the world-spirit. This universal mode in which the principle comes forth and permeates the present is the true one; what was wrong was the fact that the principle came forth as the peculiar possession of one individual.

(i. 444)

It appears, then, that the condemnation of Socrates arises from the clash between the legitimate demands of collective (*Sittlichkeit*) and individual morality (*Moralität*), which in turn reflects a stage in human development in which the collective and the individual are separate and therefore potentially conflicting. This stage is to be superseded by a higher stage of development in which the individual and the collective are somehow identified, not by the subordination of one to the other, nor by the merging of the individual in the collective, but by the development of a higher form of individuality in which individuality is constituted by its role in the collective.

Kierkegaard discusses Socrates extensively in one of his earliest works, *The Concept of Irony, with Continual Reference to Socrates*. This was his MA thesis, submitted to the University of Copenhagen in 1841, shortly before the major crisis of his life, his breaking off his engagement to Regine Olsen. (The examiners' reports are preserved in the university records, giving an amusing picture of the problems of the academic mind confronted with wayward talent.) His treatment of Socrates is Hegelian: for him as for Hegel Socrates stands at a turning-point in world history, in which the world-spirit advances to a higher stage of development, and for him too that breakthrough demands the sacrifice of the individual. 'An individual may be world-historically justified and yet unauthorized. Insofar as he is the latter he must become a sacrifice; insofar as he is the former he must prevail, that is, he must prevail by becoming a sacrifice' (260).[11] For Kierkegaard as for Hegel the role of Socrates is to lead Greek morality to a higher stage of development; what is original in his treatment is his identification of irony as the means by which this transformation of morality was to be effected. Classical Hellenism had outlived itself, but before a new principle could appear all the false preconceptions of outmoded morality had to be cleared away. That was Socrates' role, and irony was the weapon which he employed:

> [I]rony is the glaive, the two-edged sword, that he swung like an avenging angel over Greece ... [I]rony is the very incitement of subjectivity, and in Socrates this is truly a world-historical passion. In Socrates one process ends and with him a new one begins. He is the last classical figure, but he consumes this sterling quality and natural fullness of his in the divine service by which he destroys classicism.
>
> (211–12)

By irony Kierkegaard does not mean pretended ignorance or a pose of deference to others. 'Irony' is given a technical sense, taken over from Hegel, of 'infinite, absolute negativity'. What this amounts to is the supersession of the lower stage in a dialectical process in favour of the higher. Kierkegaard gives the example of the supersession of Judaism by Christianity, in which John the Baptist has an 'ironical' role comparable with that of Socrates: '[H]e [i.e. John] let Judaism continue to exist and at the same time developed the seeds of its own downfall within it' (268). But there was a crucial difference between Socrates and John, in that the latter lacked consciousness of his irony:

> [F]or the ironic formation to be perfectly developed, it is required that the subject also become conscious of his irony, feel negatively free as he passes judgment on the given actuality and enjoy this negative freedom.
>
> (ibid.)

This condition was fulfilled by Socrates, who was the first person to exhibit irony as 'a qualification of subjectivity':

> If irony is a qualification of subjectivity, it must exhibit itself the first time subjectivity makes its appearance in world history. Irony is,

namely, the first and most abstract qualification of subjectivity. This points to the historical turning point where subjectivity made its appearance for the first time, and with this we come to Socrates.

(281)

So Socrates' contribution to the development of morality is consciously to reject the authority of all previous moral norms and to be aware of his freedom. The pretended objective authority of these norms is superseded by their subjective acceptance by the individual. So, irony amounts not to moral nihilism, but to moral subjectivism. The connection with irony in the normal sense seems to be twofold: first, that the pretence of ignorance by Socrates was, in Kierkegaard's view, a tactic which he used in his destructive critique of conventional morality, and secondly, that the ironic individual no longer takes morality seriously. He cannot take conventional morality seriously because he has exploded its claims to objectivity. But he cannot take his self-adopted morality seriously either because he looks on it as a task which he has arbitrarily set himself, something perhaps like a hobby which one has just chosen to take up (235). Kierkegaard gives no indication of the answer to the question why the ironist should not simply give up morality altogether; he describes Socrates as arriving 'at the idea of the good, the beautiful, the true only as the boundary, that is com[ing] up to ideal infinity as possibility' (197), which seems to hint at some yet higher level in which moral subjectivism is itself superseded. A comparison earlier in the book (29) between the magnetic effect of Socrates on his acquaintances and Christ's imparting the Holy Spirit to his disciples may point towards the later works in which this higher level is found in the leap of faith, but in this work this remains the merest suggestion.

The suggestion is developed considerably in Kierkegaard's *Concluding Unscientific Postscript* (1846), where the traditional picture of Socrates as a forerunner of Christianity is given a characteristically idiosyncratic turn. The essence of Christianity is now seen as subjectivity. From the objective standpoint of speculative philosophy Christianity is an absurdity, which can be embraced only by the criterionless leap of faith on the part of the individual, a leap which is not the acceptance of an abstract system of propositions, but a personal commitment to a way of life. This subjective commitment transcends objective knowledge, and is held by Kierkegaard to give access to a unique form of truth:

> *An objective uncertainty held fast in an approximation-process of the most passionate inwardness is the truth*, the highest truth attainable for an existing individual [Kierkegaard's emphasis] . . . [T]he above definition of truth is an equivalent expression for faith. Without risk there is no faith. Faith is precisely the contradiction between the infinite passion of the individual's inwardness and the objective uncertainty. If I am capable of grasping God objectively, I do not believe, but precisely because I cannot do this I must believe. If I wish to preserve myself in faith I must constantly be intent on holding fast the objective uncertainty, so as to remain out upon the deep, over seventy thousand fathoms of water, still preserving my faith.

$(182)^{12}$

In his subjective adherence to morality Socrates came as near to this truth as was possible for a pagan:

> In the principle that subjectivity, inwardness, is the truth, there is comprehended the Socratic wisdom, whose everlasting merit it was to have become aware of the essential significance of existence, of the fact that the knower is an existing individual. For this reason Socrates was in the truth by virtue of his ignorance, in the highest sense in which this was possible within paganism.

(183)

Further, Kierkegaard is prepared to attribute to Socrates not only subjective commitment to morality, but also subjective faith in God, a faith which foreshadows indeed the faith of the Christian, while lacking its deeply paradoxical character:

> When Socrates believed that there was a God, he held fast to the objective uncertainty with the whole passion of his inwardness, and it is precisely in this contradiction and in this risk, that faith is rooted. Now it is otherwise. Instead of the objective uncertainty, there is here a certainty, that objectively it is absurd; and this absurdity, held fast in the passion of inwardness, is faith. The Socratic ignorance is as a witty jest in comparison with the earnestness of facing the absurd; and the Socratic existential inwardness is as Greek light-mindedness in comparison with the grave strenuosity of faith.
>
> (188)

So Socrates combines subjective conviction in the existence of God with the view that objectively the truth of the matter is uncertain. To the extent that that position involves some intellectual discomfort it is a mere approximation to the genuine anguish of the Christian, whose commitment is to truths concerning which it is objectively certain that they are absurd.

For Nietzsche, Socrates was one of a number of figures, including also Christ and Wagner, for whom he had profoundly ambivalent feelings: as he said, 'Socrates is so close to me that I am nearly always fighting him.' This ambivalence finds expression in differences of tone, sometimes between different works, sometimes in the same work. His presentation of Socrates in his first published work, *The Birth of Tragedy* (1872), illustrates this. The central thesis of this work is that Greek tragedy arose from the interaction of two opposed aspects of the creativity of the Greeks, which Nietzsche terms the Apollonian and the Dionysian. The Apollonian tendency, which has its purest expression in Homer, is characterized rather obscurely via an analogy with dreaming; it seems to amount to the presentation of an imaginary world, specifically the world of the Homeric gods, in a lucid and delightful form. The Dionysian tendency, whose analogue is intoxication, is the tendency to give expression to ecstatic and excitable impulses, especially sexual impulses and impulses to violence. Religious festivals were the traditional occasions on which these impulses were allowed expression, and it was the unique achievement of the Greeks to develop a form of festival, the dramatic festival, in which the marriage of these two tendencies gave rise to an art form, tragedy, which combines Apollonian illusion and Dionysian excitement in a unique synthesis. The Apollonian element is associated particularly with the episodes of dialogue in Attic tragedy, and the Dionysian with the chorus, but we must not think of the synthesis as simple juxtaposition. Rather (though the obscurity of Nietzsche's writing renders interpretation hazardous), the basic idea is that the world of tragedy is at once as dark and terrible as the Dionysian forces and as lucid and, in a mysterious way, joyful as the sunlit world of the Homeric gods. 'So extraordinary is the power of the epic-Apollonian that before our eyes it transforms the most terrible things by the joy in mere appearance and in redemption through mere appearance' (12).[13]

This synthesis, achieved in the dramas of Aeschylus and Sophocles, disappears in the work of Euripides; Euripidean tragedy is a degenerate form, whose distinctive feature is a realistic depiction of character, closer to the world of New Comedy than to the terrifying yet ideal world of Aeschylus and Sophocles. Nietzsche's term for this is that Euripides

> brought the spectator onto the stage . . . Through him the everyday man forced his way from the spectators' seats onto the stage; the mirror in which formerly only grand and bold traits were represented now showed the painful fidelity that conscientiously reproduces even the botched outlines of nature.
>
> (11)

It is this which brings Socrates onto the scene, since Nietzsche, echoing in his idiosyncratic fashion the ancient tradition that Socrates had collaborated with Euripides (DL, 2.18), sees him as a decisive influence in the degeneration of tragedy which he saw Euripides as having effected.

Once again, the precise form of this influence is not easy to recover from Nietzsche's prose. He speaks of Euripides as being only a mask through which speaks a new demonic power, neither Dionysus nor Apollo, but Socrates (*Birth of Tragedy* 12). The literal meaning hinted at appears to be this, that Euripidean realism is founded on psychological naturalism. Dramatic characters have to be shown acting on the same psychological principles which we use to explain the actions of actual people in everyday life. This is what Nietzsche calls '*aesthetic Socratism* [author's emphasis], whose supreme law reads roughly as follows "To be beautiful is to be intelligible" as the counterpart of the Socratic dictum "Knowledge is virtue"' (11). So 'Socratism' seems to be the name for a spirit of naturalistic rationalism, which seeks to tame the terrible forces so gloriously exhibited in Aeschylus and Sophocles by subjecting them to elucidation and criticism.

> Socratism condemns existing art as well as existing ethics. Wherever Socratism turns its searching eyes it sees lack of insight and the power of illusion; and from this lack it infers the essential perversity and reprehensibility of what exists. Basing himself on this point, Socrates conceives it to be his duty to correct existence: all alone, with an expression of irreverence and superiority, as the precursor of an altogether different culture, art and morality, he enters a world, to touch whose very hem would give us the greatest happiness.
>
> (13)

Aesthetic Socratism seems thus to be the extension to the realm of art of the intellectualism which the Platonic Socrates seeks to apply to conduct. For the Platonic Socrates virtue is knowledge and is sufficient for *eudaimonia*; *so* the good life is to be achieved through understanding, and all wrongdoing is to be attributed to lack of understanding. Just as the Platonic Socrates gives no positive role to the non-rational elements in the personality, so Socratic art has no room for the mysterious, for what cannot be captured by theory. But it is precisely its resistance to theory which gives tragedy its power and profundity. It explores forces which transcend psychological understanding, and it exhibits dilemmas which it is beyond the power of moral theory to resolve. Socratism thus represents a profound impoverishment of the spirit, which Nietzsche calls (using the French term) *décadence*.

The use of this term brings out the ambivalence in Nietzsche's attitude to Socrates. *The Birth of Tragedy* is pervaded by a sense both of the superhuman quality of the individual person Socrates, 'the human being whom knowledge and reasons have liberated from the fear of death' (15), and of the transcending power of the spirit of enquiry which that person represents. The 'pleasure of Socratic insight' transforms one's whole attitude to the world:

> the Platonic Socrates will appear as the teacher of an altogether new form of 'Greek cheerfulness' and blissful affirmation of existence that seeks to discharge itself in actions-most often in maieutic and educational influences on noble youths, with a view to eventually producing a genius.
>
> (ibid.)

> [W]e cannot *fail* to see in Socrates the one turning point and vortex of so-called world history
>
> (ibid.)

since Socrates is the incarnation of the scientific spirit, which has led to the heights of modern scientific achievement, and without which humanity might not even have survived. But at the same time Nietzsche is convinced that this sense of Socratic optimism, this faith in the power of the intellect to solve all problems of conduct and of nature, is not only a profound delusion, but also a symptom of degeneration. Later sections of *The Birth of Tragedy* express this strongly:

> From this intrinsically degenerate music [*namely, the New Attic Dithyramb, a musical form developed in the late fifth century BC*] the genuinely musical natures turned away with the same repugnance that they felt for the art-destroying tendency of Socrates. The unerring instinct of Aristophanes was surely right when it included Socrates himself, the tragedy of Euripides, and the music of the New Dithyrambic poets in the same feeling of hatred, recognizing in all three phenomena the signs of a degenerate culture.
>
> (17)

> One is chained by the Socratic love of knowledge and the delusion of being able thereby to heal the eternal wound of existence.
>
> (18)

Later in the same section he speaks of the modern world as entangled in the net of Alexandrian (i.e. uncreative and scholastic) culture, proposing as its ideal the theoretical man labouring in the service of science, whose archetype is Socrates, and of the fruit of Socratic culture as 'optimism, with its delusion of limitless power'. The 'Attempt at a Self-Criticism' added to the second edition of the work fourteen years later returns to this theme: '[Tl]hat of which tragedy died, the Socratism of morality, the dialectics, frugality and cheerfulness of the theoretical man . . . might not this very Socratism be a sign of decline, of weariness, of infection, of the anarchical dissolution of the instincts?' (1).

In later writings, particularly those written in 1888, shortly before his final mental collapse, the tone is harsher. Nietzsche now identifies himself with the Dionysian forces, and sees Socrates' rejection of them as in effect a personal rejection, to which he responds with extreme emotional violence. In the section of *Ecce Homo* devoted to *The Birth of Tragedy* he says that that work's two decisive novelties are first, the understanding of the Dionysian phenomenon, now seen as 'the sole root of the whole of Hellenic art', and secondly, 'the understanding of Socratism: Socrates for the first time recognized as an agent of Hellenic disintegration, as a typical *décadent*'. 'I was the first to see', he continues,

> the real antithesis – the *degenerated* instinct which turns against life with subterranean vengeance. . . and a formula of *supreme affirmation* born out of fullness, of superfluity, an affirmation without reservation even of suffering, even of guilt . . . This ultimate, joyfullest, boundlessly exuberant Yes to life is not only the highest insight, it is also the *profoundest*, the insight most strictly confirmed and maintained by truth and knowledge . . . Recognition, affirmation of reality is for the strong man as great a necessity as is for the weak man, under the inspiration of weakness, cowardice and *flight* in the face of reality – the 'ideal' . . . They are not at liberty to know: *décadents need* the lie – it is one of the conditions of their existence – He who not only understands the word 'dionysian' but understands *himself* in the word 'dionysian' needs no refutation of Plato or of Christianity or of Schopenhauer – *he smells the decomposition*.
>
> (80)[14]

The language of sickness and decomposition takes up the theme of the essay on Socrates in *The Twilight of the Idols*, written earlier that year. Nietzsche begins with Socrates' last words, which he interprets as an expression of thanks for release from the sickness of life (see above). But the world-weariness which this expresses is itself the sickness from which Socrates suffers along with all so-called sages who theorize about morality and value.

> 'Here at any rate there must be something *sick*' – this is *our* retort: one ought to take a closer look at them, those wisest of every age! . . . Does

wisdom perhaps appear on earth as a raven which is inspired by the smell of carrion?

(39)[15]

Socrates and Plato are 'symptoms of decay . . . agents of the dissolution of Greece. . . pseudo-Greek . . . anti-Greek', in that their theorizing involves a negative attitude to life, in opposition to the triumphant affirmation of the Dionysian man with whom Nietzsche has identified himself.

But Nietzsche does not stop at the characterization of Socrates as a typical (perhaps the archetypal) *décadent*; in five astonishing sections (3–7) he mounts a ferocious attack on the individual personality of Socrates, in terms expressive of a loathsome snobbishness which even slips into anti-Semitism. Socrates belonged to the lowest social class: he was riff-raff. His ugliness was a symptom of a foul and dissolute temperament. Was he even a Greek at all? Dialectic is a malicious device by which the rabble defeat their betters, people of finer taste and better manners. It is a weapon of last resort in the hands of those who have no other defence. (That is why the Jews were dialecticians.) Socrates was a buffoon who got himself taken seriously.

Reading this stuff with hindsight, in the knowledge of Nietzsche's imminent breakdown, one is inclined to dismiss it as pathological raving. Yet this violence, pathological though it may be, is itself an expression of Nietzsche's deep ambivalence towards Socrates. In section 8 he says that what has gone before indicates the way in which Socrates could repel, which makes it all the more necessary to explain his fascination. So sections 3–7 present an adverse reaction to Socrates, leaving it ambiguous how far Nietzsche himself shares it. In some sense, no doubt, the reaction is his, but then so is what follows. The grotesque caricature of those sections is counterbalanced by a dignified portrait of Socrates as someone who attempted, misguidedly indeed, but seriously and with benevolent intent, to cure the ills of his age by subjecting the dangerous Dionysian impulses to the control of reason. Nietzsche does not withdraw his negative evaluation; Socrates 'seemed to be a physician, a saviour', but his faith in rationality at any cost was error and self-deception: 'Socrates was a misunderstanding: *the entire morality of improvement, the Christian included, has been a misunderstanding.*' Yet the change of voice is most striking, and the return to the theme of Socrates' death in the final section has a genuinely elegiac tone:

> Did he himself grasp that [sc. *that so long as life is ascending, happiness and instinct are one*], this shrewdest of all self-deceivers? Did he at last say that to himself in the *wisdom* of his courage for death? . . . Socrates *wanted* to die – it was not Athens, it was *he* who handed himself the poison cup, who compelled Athens to hand him the poison cup . . . 'Socrates is no physician,' he said softly to himself: 'death alone is a physician here . . . Socrates himself has only been a long time sick . . .'.
>
> (44)

Even to the end, it appears, Nietzsche fought against Socrates because he was so close to him.

Chapter 6
Conclusion

Every age has to recreate its own Socrates. What is his significance for a post-Christian, post-idealist epoch for whom neither the figure of a precursor of Christ nor that of the embodiment of the world-spirit in its development of a higher form of consciousness has any meaning? One answer is to view his significance historically, as a pioneer of systematic ethical thought, as a central influence on Plato, as the focus of Socratic literature, and so on. But the historical importance of Socrates, unquestionable though it is, does not exhaust his significance, even for a secular, non-ideological age such as ours. As well as a historical person and a literary persona, Socrates is in many ways an exemplary figure, a figure which challenges, encourages, and inspires. To take the most obvious instance, Socrates still presents a challenge to those whose way into philosophy, and more generally into systematic critical thinking, is via the Socratic dialogues. Even in a world where the study of the ancient classics has lost its cultural pre-eminence, many find that those dialogues, whose comparative absence of technicality and conversational vividness draw the reader into his or her own dialogue with the text, provide the best introduction to philosophy. Again, virtually everyone whose business is teaching finds some affinity with the Socratic method of challenging the student to examine his or her beliefs, to revise them in the light of argument, and to arrive at answers through critical reflection on the information presented. But the critical method is no mere pedagogical strategy; it is, in real life as much as in the Socratic dialogues, a method of self-criticism. The slogan 'The unexamined life is not worth living for a human being' (Pl. *Apol.* 38a) expresses a central human value, partly constitutive of integrity: namely, the willingness to rethink one's own assumptions, and thereby to reject the standing tendency to complacent dogmatism. Carried to excess, self-examination can be paralyzing, but Socrates stands as an example of a life in which it is a positive force on a heroic scale, since it produces the confidence to adhere, come what may, to those ideals which have withstood the test of self-criticism. As long as intellectual and moral integrity are human ideals, Socrates will be an appropriate exemplar of them.

References

1. *A History of Greek Philosophy*, iii (Cambridge, 1969), 372.

2. See Pl. *Gorg.* 473e, with commentary by E. R. Dodds, *Plato* Gorgias (Oxford, 1959), 247–8.

3. For details see J. Barnes, 'Editor's Notes', *Phronesis*, 32 (1987), 325–6.

4. For details see P. A. Vander Waerdt, 'Socratic Justice and Self-Sufficiency: The Story of the Delphic Oracle in Xenophon's *Apology of Socrates', Oxford Studies in Ancient Philosophy*, 11 (1993), 1–48.

5. For a useful summary of the evidence see C. H. Kahn, *Plato and the Socratic Dialogue* (Cambridge, 1996), ch. 2.

6. I argue briefly for this general claim in *Plato*, Protagoras (2nd edn.; Oxford, 1991), pp. xiv–xvi, and more fully for specific instances of it in ch. 4 of this volume.

7. The objection is urged by G. Vlastos in 'Socrates on "The Parts of Virtue"', in his *Platonic Studies* (2nd edn.; Princeton, NJ, 1981).

8. The example is borrowed from T. C. Brickhouse and N. D. Smith, *Plato's Socrates* (New York and Oxford, 1994), 69–71.

9. For further information see I. Alon, *Socrates in Mediaeval Arabic Literature* (Leiden and Jerusalem, 1991).

10. *Lectures on the History of Philosophy*, tr. E. S. Haldane (London, 1982).

11. *The Concept of Irony, with Continual Reference to Socrates*, tr. H. V. Hong and E. H. Hong (Princeton, NJ, 1989).

12. *Concluding Unscientific Postscript*, tr. D. F. Swenson and W. Lowrie (Princeton, NJ, 1941).
13. *The Birth of Tragedy*, tr. W. Kaufmann (New York, 1967).
14. *Ecce Homo*, tr. R. J. Hollingdale (Harmondsworth, 1992).
15. *The Twilight of the Idols*, tr. R. J. Hollingdale (Harmondsworth, 1990).

Further Reading

Ancient Sources

All the dialogues of Plato cited in this book are available in numerous English translations. The most accessible translation of the Socratic writings of Xenophon is that by H. Tredennick and R. Waterfield, *Xenophon, Conversations of Socrates* in Penguin Classics (Harmondsworth, 1990), which has an excellent introduction and notes. The Socratic works are also available as part of the Loeb Classical Library edition of Xenophon (Greek with facing English translation), *Memorabilia* and *Oeconomicus* translated by E. C. Marchant (London and New York, 1923), *Symposium* and *Apology* translated by O. J. Todd (London and Cambridge, Mass., 1961). Diogenes Laertius' *Lives of the Philosophers* is also available in the Loeb edition (2 vols., tr. R. D. Hicks (Cambridge, Mass., 1925)). Aristophanes' *Clouds* is translated by B. B. Rogers (London, 1916 (repr. 1924 as part of the complete Loeb edition of Aristophanes)) and by W. Arrowsmith (Ann Arbor, Mich., 1962). The edition of the play by K. J. Dover (Oxford, 1968, abridged edn., 1970) contains a comprehensive introduction which is very useful even to those who have no Greek.

Most of the fragments of the minor Socratic writers are available in Greek only; the standard edition is that by G. Giannantoni, *Socratis et Socraticorum Reliquiae*, 4 vols. (Naples, 1991). The principal fragments of Aeschines are translated in G. C. Field, *Plato and his Contemporaries* (London, 1930), ch. 11.

J. Ferguson, *Socrates, A Source Book* (London, 1970) contains a
comprehensive collection of passages of ancient works (in English
translation) referring to Socrates.

Modern Works

The modern literature on Socrates is vast. T. C. Brickhouse and N. D.
Smith, *Socrates on Trial* (Oxford, 1989) contains a useful guide to it
(pp. 272–316). This note restricts itself to major works in English.

Comprehensive Survey

Guthrie, W. K. C., *A History of Greek Philosophy,* iii, part 2 (Cambridge,
1969). Published separately 1971 under title *Socrates*.

Biography

Taylor, A. E., *Varia Socratica* (Oxford, 1911).

Critical and Analytical Works Concentrating on Plato's Presentation of Socrates

Brickhouse, T. C. and Smith, N. D., *Plato's Socrates* (New York and
Oxford, 1994).
Irwin, T., *Plato's Ethics* (New York and Oxford, 1995), chs. 1–9.
Santas, G. X., *Socrates* (London, Boston, and Henley, 1979).
Vlastos, G., Socrates, Ironist and Moral Philosopher (Cambridge, 1991).
——, *Socratic Studies* (ed. M. Burnyeat) (Cambridge, 1994).

Works on Socrates' Trial

Brickhouse, T. C. and Smith, N. D., *Socrates on Trial* (Oxford, 1989). A
heavy work of scholarship.
Stone, I. F., *The Trial of Socrates* (London, 1988). A lively presentation,
unreliable in places.

Collections of Articles

Benson, H. H. (ed.), *Essays on the Philosophy of Socrates* (New York and
Oxford, 1992).

Gower, B. S. and Stokes, M. C. (eds.), *Socratic Questions* (London and New York, 1992).

Prior, W. T. (ed.), *Socrates*, 4 vols. (London and New York, 1996). A comprehensive collection.

Vlastos, G. (ed.), *The Philosophy of Socrates* (Garden City, NY, 1971).

Works on Socratic Literature

Kahn, C. H., *Plato and the Socratic Dialogue* (Cambridge, 1996), chs. 1–4.

Rutherford, R. B., *The Art of Plato* (London, 1995).

Vander Waerdt, P. A., (ed.), *The Socratic Movement* (Ithaca, NY and London, 1994).

Socrates in Later Thought

Montuori, M., *Socrates: Physiology of a Myth* (Amsterdam, 1981).

Index of Ancient Works Cited

Socrates

General Index

Socrates

General Index

Expand your collection of
VERY SHORT INTRODUCTIONS

Visit the
VERY SHORT
INTRODUCTIONS
Web site

www.oup.co.uk/vsi

- ➤ **Information** about all published titles

- ➤ News of **forthcoming books**

- ➤ **Extracts** from the books, including titles
  not yet published

- ➤ **Reviews** and views

- ➤ **Links** to other **web sites** and main
  OUP web page

- ➤ Information about **VSIs in translation**

- ➤ **Contact** the editors

- ➤ **Order** other **VSIs** on-line

CLASSICS
A Very Short Introduction
Mary Beard and John Henderson

This Very Short Introduction to Classics links a haunting temple on a lonely mountainside to the glory of ancient Greece and the grandeur of Rome, and to Classics within modern culture – from Jefferson and Byron to Asterix and Ben-Hur.

'The authors show us that Classics is a "modern" and sexy subject. They succeed brilliantly in this regard … nobody could fail to be informed and entertained – and the accent of the book is provocative and stimulating.'

John Godwin, *Times Literary Supplement*

'Statues and slavery, temples and tragedies, museum, marbles, and mythology – this provocative guide to the Classics demystes its varied subject-matter while seducing the reader with the obvious enthusiasm and pleasure which mark its writing.'

Edith Hall

www.oup.co.uk/vsi/classics

ANCIENT PHILOSOPHY
A Very Short Introduction

Julia Annas

The tradition of ancient philosophy is a long, rich and varied one, in which a constant note is that of discussion and argument. This book aims to introduce readers to some ancient debates and to get them to engage with the ancient developments of philosophical themes. Getting away from the presentation of ancient philosophy as a succession of Great Thinkers, the book aims to give readers a sense of the freshness and liveliness of ancient philosophy, and of its wide variety of themes and styles.

'Incisive, elegant, and full of the excitement of doing philosophy, Julia Annas's Short Introduction boldly steps outside of conventional chronological ways of organizing material about the Greeks and Romans to get right to the heart of the human problems that exercised them, problems ranging from the relation between reason and emotion to the objectivity of truth. I can't think of a better way to begin.'

Martha Nussbaum, University of Chicago

www.oup.co.uk/vsi/ancientphilosophy

ARISTOTLE
A Very Short Introduction
Jonathan Barnes

The influence of Aristotle, the prince of philosophers, on the intellectual history of the West is second to none. In this book Jonathan Barnes examines Aristotle's scientific research, his discoveries in logic, his metaphysical theories, his work in psychology, ethics, and politics, and his ideas about art and poetry, placing his teachings in their historical context.

> 'With compressed verve, Jonathan Barnes displays the extraordinary Versatility of Aristotle, the great systematising empiricist.'
>
> **Sunday Times**

www.oup.co.uk/isbn/0-19-285408-9